Preface

Randall L. Jones and Bernard Spolsky

The 1974 Washington Language Testing Symposium was the natural result of cooperation between two recently established groups whose primary concern is language testing. The Testing Subcommittee of the United States Government Interagency Language Roundtable was organized in 1972. Its principal function is to coordinate research and development of language tests among the various U.S. Government language schools. The Commission on Language Tests and Testing was formed at the Third International Congress of Applied Linguistics in Copenhagen in August 1973 as part of the International Association of Applied Linguistics. Among the tasks assigned to the Commission was "to organize specialized meetings on tests and testing at a time other than the regular AILA Congress." In filling this task, it attempted to provide a continuation to a series of conferences on language testing which had already taken place, including the 1967 ATESL Seminar on Testing (Wigglesworth 1967), the 1967 Michigan conference (Upshur and Fata 1968), and the 1968 conference at the University of Southern California (Brière 1969). The first such meeting was organized in conjunction with the 1973 TESOL Convention; some of the papers presented there have just been published (Palmer and Spolsky 1975). A second meeting was held in Hasselt, Belgium in September 1973.

The papers in this volume represent the third of these meetings. The participants were language testing specialists from academic institutions, research centers, and U.S. and other government agencies. The primary focus of the symposium was language proficiency testing, especially as it relates to the use of foreign languages on the job. This volume includes not only the papers that were presented, but also much of the discussion that followed each paper. It thus provides a useful picture of the state of language proficiency testing, and illustrates as well the possibilities which emerge when practitioners and theorists meet to discuss their common problems.

Many people contributed to the success of the conference. Special thanks are due to the members of the Testing Subcommittee of the U.S. Government Interagency Language Roundtable who contributed financial support (the Foreign Service Institute of the Department of State; the Defense Language Institute of the Department of Defense; the Office of Education of the Department of Health, Education and Welfare; the Central Intelligence Agency; and the National Security

Agency), to Georgetown University for hosting the conference, to the Center for Applied Linguistics for their financial support as well as their willingness to publish the proceedings, and to all the participants, many of whom came from great distances to be present. We are most grateful to Allene Guss Grognet and Marcia E. Taylor of the Center for Applied Linguistics for the great assistance they provided in preparing this volume for publication.

REFERENCES

Brière, Eugene. "Current Trends in Second Language Testing." *TESOL Quarterly* 3:4 (December 1969), 333-340.

Wigglesworth, David C. (ed.). *Selected Conference Papers of the Association of Teachers of English as a Second Language.* Washington, D.C.: NAFSA, 1967.

Upshur, John A. and Julia Fata (eds.). *Problems in Foreign Language Testing. Language Learning,* Special Issue No. 3 (1968).

Palmer, Leslie and Bernard Spolsky (eds.). *Papers on Language Testing 1967-74.* Washington, D.C.: TESOL, 1975.

Table of Contents

Testing Language Proficiency in the United States Government

Randall L. Jones

Of the thousands of students enrolled in foreign language courses in the United States, only a relatively small percentage are associated with Government language training programs. Yet this minor segment of the language learning population is unusual and potentially significant for the language teaching profession as a whole. The students in U.S. Government language schools are exclusively adults who are learning a language because it is important for a position they are either occupying or are about to be placed in. Many of them have already learned a second language and have used it in the country where it is spoken. They are probably enrolled in full-time courses which last for six to twelve months. And perhaps most important, the majority of them will have occasion to use the language frequently soon after the end of the training period. The conditions for language learning are close to ideal, and certainly useful for doing research and experimentation.

Positions in federal agencies for which knowledge of a second language is required are referred to as "language-essential." Because the degree of proficiency does not need to be the same for all positions, it is necessary to define levels of proficiency and to state the minimum level for any language-essential position. Such a system obviously necessitates a testing program that can accurately assess the ability of an individual to speak, understand, read or write a foreign language, and that can assign a proficiency score to that person which will indicate whether he is qualified to assume a specified language-essential position. The outcome of such a test may well have a significant affect on the career of the individual.

In 1968 an ad hoc interagency committee (with representatives from the Foreign Service Institute [FSI], the Defense Language Institute [DLI], the National Security Agency [NSA], the Central Intelligence Agency [CIA], and the Civil Service Commission [CSC]) met to discuss the standardization of language scores for government agencies. The committee proposed a system which would provide for the recording of language proficiency in four skills: speaking, listening comprehension, reading and writing. It was decided that degrees of proficiency in each of these skills could be represented on an eleven point scale, from 0 to 5, with pluses for levels 0 through 4. A set of definitions was prepared for the four skills at each of the principal levels (1-5). (The definition for speaking is essentially the same as had already been in use at FSI prior to 1968.)

The scale and definition proposed by the ad hoc committee have been adopted by the members of the Interagency Language Roundtable of the United States Government for use in their respective language training programs. However, a number of questions relating to standards of testing, test development, test technique, test validation, etc. still remain to be answered. The Roundtable's recently established Subcommittee on Testing has been given the task of dealing with these problems, many of which are certainly not peculiar to government language programs and are, of course, not new to the language teaching profession as a whole. We felt that it was therefore appropriate to convene a meeting of both government and non-government language testing specialists to discuss them. The members of the panel possess broad and varied backgrounds in the field of language testing. They represent government-affiliated language programs as well as academic institutions in the United States, Canada and Europe. Our focus is narrow. We will not be discussing language testing in all of its forms, but only the testing of language proficiency—an individual's demonstrable competence to use a language skill of one type or another, regardless of how he may have acquired it.

In planning for the symposium we had four objectives in mind: (1) to determine the state of the art of language proficiency testing within the U.S. Government, (2) to discuss common problems relating to language testing, (3) to explore new ideas and techniques for testing, and (4) to establish a future direction for research and development. We are not operating under the delusion that any of these objectives will be completely met. It simply will not be possible to surface and discuss *all* of theproblems concerning language proficiency testing, let alone find adequate solutions for them. Furthermore, we realize that although we are dealing with an imperfect system, it may not be possible to alter it a great deal under the circumstances. We will simply have to learn to live with some of its imperfections. But we also feel an obligation to review our program carefully and to attempt to make improvements where it is possible to do so. We are optimistic that new ideas will emerge from this forum which will aid all of us in devising more accurate means of testing language proficiency.

The three skills which are most often tested at Government language schools are speaking, listening comprehension and reading. You will recall that the scores on our proficiency tests are supposed to in some way reflect language competence as described by the Civil Service definitions. In order to clarify the criteria for evaluation we are dealing with, I will give the definitions for level 3, or the minimum professional level, for each of the three skills:

The level "3" speaker should be:

> Able to speak the language with sufficient structural accuracy and vocabulary to participate effectively in most formal and informal conversations on practical, social, and professional topics. Can discuss particular interests and special fields of competence with reasonable ease; comprehension is quite complete for a normal rate of speech; vocabulary is broad enough that he rarely has to grope for a word; accent may be obviously foreign; control of grammar good; errors never interfere with understanding and rarely disturb the native speaker.

In terms of listening comprehension, the individual at level "3" is:

> Able to understand the essentials of all speech in a standard dialect, including technical discussions within a special field. Has effective understanding of face-to-face speech, delivered with normal clarity and speed in a standard dialect, on general topics and areas of special interest; has broad enough vocabulary that he rarely has to ask for paraphrasing or explanation; can follow accurately the essentials of conversations between educated native speakers, reasonably clear telephone calls, radio broadcasts, and public addresses on non-technical subjects; can understand without difficulty all forms of standard speech concerning a special professional field.

At the "3" level for reading proficiency, a person is:

> Able to read standard newspaper items addressed to the general reader, routine correspondence, reports and technical material in his special field. Can grasp the essentials of articles of the above types without using a dictionary; for accurate understanding moderately frequent use of a dictionary is required. Has occasional difficulty with unusually complex structures and low-frequency idioms.

If these definitions are to be taken seriously, we must be satisfied that anyone who is tested and assigned a proficiency rating can meet the criteria for that level. One of the principal problems we are faced with is the construction of proficiency tests which measure language ability accurately enough to correspond to these definitions. At the present time there are several kinds of language proficiency tests used in the various agencies, i.e. different tests are used to measure the same skill because of differing circumstances. In some cases we feel confident that the correlation between the performance on the test and the performance in a real-life situation is good. In other cases we are less certain, mainly because no validation studies have been made with the definitions as a basis.

Speaking proficiency is tested in a direct way at FSI and the CIA by means of an Oral Interview Test. In spite of its drawbacks, this method probably provides the most valid measurement of general speaking proficiency currently available. Research which is now in progress indicates that the reliability of the oral interview test is also very good. But it has certain disadvantages with respect to its administration. It is expensive and limited in that trained testers must be present to administer it. There is often a need to test large populations or to give a test at a location to which it would not be economically feasible to send a testing team. What are the alternatives? There are several tests of speaking proficiency now available which are not limited by these restrictions, but unfortunately they do not provide a sufficiently adequate measurement for our purposes. For example, most structured oral language tests use a text, pictures or a recording as the stimulus. The response of the examinee is limited and often unnatural. There is little possibility for variation. It is somewhat similar to doing archaeological field work by looking at black and white snapshots of the site. You can get an idea, but you cannot explore. There is also the possibility of inferring a speaking proficiency level on the basis of a listening comprehension test, but we do not yet have convincing data to show that a high enough correlation exists between the two types of tests. We are still looking—and should continue to look—for alternate means of testing speaking proficiency.

Because the requirements for language use differ from agency to agency, the relative importance of testing certain skills also differs. The testing of listening comprehension provides a good example. Within the various language schools there are several kinds of listening comprehension tests, including a number of standardized multiple-choice tests of the type familiar to all of us. These tests provide the desirable element of objectivity, but they are also open to some serious questions. For example, is it really possible for a test with this format to correspond in any way to the Civil Service definitions, which are expressed in functional terms? A multiple-choice test can serve as an indicator of proficiency, but until we can validate it against performance based on the definitions, we do not know how accurate the indicator is. Multiple-choice listening comprehension tests also have certain inherent problems such as memory, distraction, double jeopardy (if both the stimulus and alternatives are in the target language) and mixed skills (i.e. the examinee may be able to understand the stimulus, but may not be able to read the alternatives). It is possible for an examinee to understand the target language quite well, yet score low on a test because of other factors. There is, unfortunately, no way to make a direct assessment of a person's ability to comprehend a foreign language short of gaining access to his language perception mechanism, whatever that is.

At FSI there is no requirement to distinguish between speaking and listening comprehension, thus the FSI S-rating is a combination of both; comprehension is one of the factors on which the S-rating is based. At the CIA a distinction is made between an S-rating and a U-rating (U = understanding), but a separate listening comprehension test is not given. In most cases the judgment about an examinee's comprehension ability is made on the basis of his performance on the oral interview. Such a method is potentially problematic if an examinee's skill in understanding the language greatly exceeds his ability to speak it. The level of language difficulty in the interview is necessarily dictated by the examinee's speaking proficiency, thus his skill for understanding what the examiner says may not be sufficiently challenged. To correct this deficiency the CIA Language Learning Center is presently experimenting with the use of taped passages as a part of the oral interview. We have yet to overcome some problems in this regard, not the least of which is the establishment of evaluation criteria.

All of the agencies have a requirement for testing reading proficiency. At FSI, and in some cases at the CIA, the last ten to fifteen minutes of the oral interview are spent in an oral translation exercise. An approximation of the examinee's reading proficiency is made on the basis of his speaking proficiency. He is then given a short passage in the target language—often taken directly from a current newspaper or magazine—which he reads and retells in English without the aid of a dictionary. The passages are scaled according to the eleven levels of proficiency, and the examinee must be able to give a good, accurate rendering in order to receive the rating which corresponds to the level of the passage. If the linguist feels that the passage was not appropriate for the examinee, he can choose a second one of greater or lesser difficulty. In a typical test three to four passages are read. This method has the advantage of being easy to administer. It is also a relatively simple matter to change the test by changing the passages, provided they are properly scaled. Unfortunately, there has never been a reliability study made of this test. Furthermore, in spite of the directness of oral translation in comparison to a multiple-choice test, it cannot yet be assumed that the examinee's performance in translating correlates directly with his ability to read and comprehend written material in the target language. Again, it will be necessary to make an exhaustive validity study before we can be assured that it does, in fact, provide an accurate measure of reading proficiency.

Multiple-choice reading proficiency tests are used on a regular basis at DLI and the CIA Language Learning Center. The objectivity and reliability provided by these standardized tests is desirable indeed, but the disadvantages must also be acknowledged. In our case, we have had only one form for each language for more than ten years. Obviously some employees have taken the test more than once, sometimes within a relatively short period of time. Validity in such cases is, of course, questionable. For this reason we are in the process of devising a new testing model which we feel is a more valid measurement of reading proficiency, and for which we plan to make multiple forms.

It may sound like heresy to some ears, but in all agencies translation tests are used in certain cases for measuring reading proficiency. However, we really have no empirical evidence about the validity, or lack of it, of such tests. The main administrative problem with this type of test is scoring. It must be done manually, and with so many possibilities for mistakes of differing magnitude it is difficult to devise a reliable method of scoring. The use of translation as a testing device should not, however, be discarded.

Within the Government language community the greatest amount of research in the area of reading proficiency testing has been done at DLI's Systems Development Agency in Monterey, California. Here a team of linguists and psychometricians is working on many of the problems of testing, especially test validity. They are also charged with the awesome responsibility of developing listening comprehension and reading tests for more than fifty languages, so a practical balance between research and development has to be maintained. Other Defense Department language programs are also occupied with the challenge of developing new kinds of reading tests and have discovered some novel, interesting techniques of getting at the problem.

The Government Accounting Office (GAO) "Report to the Congress on the Need to Improve Language Training Programs and Assignments for U.S. Government Personnel Overseas" discusses some of the problems of testing language proficiency in U.S. Government agencies and suggests that research and development of language tests be coordinated among the agencies. We cannot know how effective our language training programs are or how valid our mechanism for assigning personnel to language-essential positions is unless we are confident that our testing programs provide an accurate measurement of language proficiency. We are reasonably satisfied that our present system works; but we should not be completely content with it, as there is still much to be done.

The U.S. Government language community has had vast experience with language testing—each year more than seven thousand people are tested in approximately sixty different languages. The range of proficiency covers the entire spectrum; all the way from the beginner to those who have a command of the language equivalent to that of an educated native speaker. A large amount of data is thus generated which can be of value not only for our purposes, but for anyone interested in language testing. A cooperative effort on the part of Government and non-Government language interests would therefore be of great mutual benefit.

Since the Government has such a large stake in improved testing, should we not dedicate a greater portion of our resources to research, in order to learn more about the tests we are presently using, as well as to experiment with new techniques? Perhaps this symposium will be the stimulus to initiate a comprehensive program of evaluation, research and development in language proficiency testing.

DISCUSSION

Lado: I think the paper was very helpful in giving us a broad presentation of many of the issues that interest us. I do not agree that the interview is more natural than some of the other forms of tests, because if I'm being interviewed and I know that my salary and my promotion depend on it, no matter how charming the interviewer and his assistants are, this couldn't be any more unnatural. I would also argue against considering Civil Service definitions as dogma. In my view they can be changed, and better definitions can be found. One further point. "We shouldn't discard translation," we were told a couple of times. I would like to discard translation, especially as a test of reading.

Jones: Any test is unnatural and is going to create anxiety, especially if one's salary or grade depends on it. As a matter of fact, just speaking a foreign language in a real-life situation can cause anxiety. As to the Civil Service definitions, they are not dogma, and they may well be changed. Finally, translation, as is the case with all reading tests, is one indirect measure of a person's ability to understand written language. It has its drawbacks, but it also has its merits.

Nickel: There is certainly a revival—a renaissance—in the interest of translation now taking place in Europe. In some work we have done we seem to see a certain correlation between a skill like speaking and translation, and I feel that translation tests are useful for skills other than translating.

Davies: You mention speaking, listening and reading level 3. I'd like to know whether level 3 for reading is supposed to be equivalent in some way to level 3 for listening. It seems to me that as you read them through very quickly, they mean very different things.

Jones: As far as the structure of the language is concerned, they should. It should not be inferred that a level 3 understander (aural) is also a level 3 reader.

Davies: In talking about reading, you said that, "the passages are scaled according to the eleven levels of proficiency." How were they scaled?

Wilds: Perhaps I can answer that question, although it began so long ago that it's hard to say how they were scaled initially. Since the beginning, new passages have been matched with old ones so that they are proven to be in an order of difficulty which seems to hold true for everybody who takes the test. A passage that is graded 3+, for example, will not be given that final grade until it is shown by several dozen examinees to match the performance on accepted 3+ passages. I might say that there are no 0 or 0+ passages as far as I know, so there are really only 9 levels. And in many languages where there aren't many tests, there are no plus ratings on the passages. You need a great many examinees to make it finer than that in gradation.

Quiñones: I'd like to add that this decision was certainly not based on the definitions, although, at least in our case, we looked at them when we were scaling the passages. Also, we made an attempt to look at the passages from the point of view of frequency of words and complexity of sentences. But ultimately it was a subjective decision by the test constructors, and the ultimate decision for keeping the passage was based on the experience of using the passages and having people at different levels handling them.

Sako: In your presentation you mentioned that the CIA was experimenting with taped passages. How far along are you on this experiment, and do you foresee an instrument that is as reliable and valid as the one you are now using? And if so, do you think there will be a substantial savings in rating people?

Jones: Our primary concern with giving a rating for listening comprehension on the basis of the oral interview is that if the person tested is able to understand the language very well, but for some reason is deficient in speaking, it is very likely that he will get a low rating for listening comprehension. There is no way for him to demonstrate that his ability to understand exceeds—in some cases by as much as two levels—his ability to speak. So our experimentation in this respect is primarily to find out whether, on the basis of the taped passages, a person might be able to understand better than is evident from the interview. We have a fairly good idea of his minimal level; the taped passages we hope will bring out anything that exceed that. Our primary problem is, once again, trying to line the passages up with our levels.

Hindmarsh: Is there a definition of writing proficiency?

Jones: Yes, there is. We rarely test writing, however, and our research and development projects are not currently concerned with any type of writing proficiency test.

Frey: I'd like to ask about the expense involved in oral testing. We found, of course, that it's very expensive. I wonder how long your tests take, and how expensive they are?

Jones: I couldn't really quote a dollar figure, but Jim Frith quotes a figure of $35.00 for a test of speaking and reading. It's a very expensive type of test because we have two testers with the examinee for a period of anywhere from 15 minutes to more than a half hour, depending on the level. A person who comes in with a 0+ level doesn't take long to test. However, if a person is up in the 4 or 4 + range, we have to take a lot more time to explore and find out where the border really is. We feel, however, that whatever the expense is, it's worth it. We have to have this kind of a test to be able to find out what a person's ability to speak really is. While it would be possible to use taped tests, if you have to take time to listen to the tape anyway, why not do it face to face in the first place?

Theoretical and Technical Considerations in Oral Proficiency Testing

John L. D. Clark

The intent of this paper is to identify and discuss some of the major theoretical and practical considerations in the development and use of oral proficiency tests. A few definitions are required in order to identify and delineate the area of discussion. A *proficiency* test is considered as any measurement procedure aimed at determining the examinee's ability to receive or transmit information in the test language for some pragmatically useful purpose within a real-life setting. For example, a test of the student's ability to comprehend various types of radio broadcasts or to understand the dialogue of a foreign language film would be considered a proficiency test in listening comprehension. A proficiency test in the area of written production would involve measuring the student's ability to produce such written documents as notes to the plumber, informal letters to acquaintances, and various types of business correspondence. In all cases, the emphasis in proficiency testing is on determining the student's ability to operate effectively in real-life language use situations.

In the testing of *oral proficiency*, possible real-life contexts include such activities as reading aloud (as in giving a prepared speech) dictating into a tape recorder, talking on the telephone, and conversing face-to-face with one or more interlocutors. In terms of the relative frequency of these speaking activities, face-to-face conversation is definitely the most highly preponderant, and with some justification, the term "oral proficiency" is usually thought of in terms of a conversational situation.

A further distinction is necessary between two major subcategories of proficiency testing: *direct* and *indirect*. In *direct* proficiency testing, the testing format and procedure attempts to duplicate as closely as possible the setting and operation of the real-life situations in which the proficiency is normally demonstrated. For example, a direct proficiency test of listening comprehension might involve the presentation of taped radio broadcasts, complete with the static and somewhat limited frequency range typical of actual radio reception. A direct proficiency test of reading comprehension would involve the use of verbatim magazine articles, newspaper reports, and other texts actually encountered in real-life reading situations. A direct test of oral proficiency, in the face-to-face communication sense, would involve a test setting in which the examinee and one or more human interlocutors do, in fact, engage in communicative dialogue. A major requirement of direct proficiency tests is that they must provide a very close facsimile or "work sample" of the real-life language situations in question, with respect to both the setting and operation of the tests and the linguistic areas and content which they embody.

Indirect proficiency tests, on the other hand, do not require the establishment of a highly face-valid and representative testing situation. In some cases, of course, an indirect test may involve certain quasi-realistic activities on the student's part. For example, in the speaking area, a test which is defined here as indirect may require the student to describe printed pictures aloud or in some other way produce intelligible spoken responses. However, since such testing procedures are not truly reflective of a real-life dialogue situation, they are considered indirect rather than direct measures of oral proficiency.

Other indirect techniques may have virtually no formal correspondence to real-life language activities. One example is the so-called "cloze" technique, in which the examinee is asked to resupply letters or words that have been systematically deleted from a continuous text. This specific behavior would rarely if ever be called for in real-life situations.

The validity of these and other indirect procedures as measures of real-life proficiency is established through statistical—specifically, correlational—means. If and when a given indirect test is found to correlate highly and consistently with more direct tests of the proficiency in question, it becomes useful as a surrogate measure of that proficiency, in the sense that it permits reasonably accurate predictions of the level of performance that the student would demonstrate if he were to undergo the more direct test. This type of correlational validity is usually referred to as *congruent* or *concurrent* validity.

In addition to being either face/content-valid or concurrently-valid, as required, direct and indirect proficiency tests must also be *reliable*, in the sense that they must provide consistent, replicable information about student performance. If no intervening learning has taken place, a given student would be expected to receive approximately the same score on a number of different administrations of the same test or alternate forms thereof. If, however, test scores are found to vary appreciably through influences other than changes in student ability, test unreliability is indicated, and the measure accordingly becomes less appropriate as a true measure of student performance.

Finally, both direct and indirect proficiency tests must have a satisfactory degree of *practicality*. No matter how highly valid and reliable a particular testing method may be, it cannot be serviceable for "real-world" applications unless it falls within acceptable limits of cost, manpower requirements, and time constraints for administration and scoring. To overlook or minimize these aspects when planning and developing testing procedures is to court serious disillusionment when the procedures go through the trial-by-fire of operational use.

We have so far defined the area of "oral proficiency testing"; identified direct and indirect techniques within this area; and outlined the three major considerations of validity, reliability, and practicality as touchstones for a more detailed analysis of specific testing procedures. In conducting this analysis, it will also be helpful to present a brief taxonomy of theoretically possible testing procedures and identify the possible procedures which most adequately fulfill the validity, reliability, and practicality criteria that have been discussed.

Two major components of any testing procedure are *administration* and *scoring*. Administration is the process by which test stimuli are presented to the examinee. "Mechanical" administration refers to procedures in which test booklets, tape recorders, videotapes, or other inanimate devices are for all practical purposes entirely responsible for test administration. Any input by a "live" examiner is restricted to peripheral matters such as giving general directions and handing out test materials. "Human" administration, on the other hand, requires the presence of a live examiner who is actively and continuously involved in the testing process: reading test questions aloud, conversing with the student in an interview situation, and so forth.

Test *scoring* is the process by which the student's responses to the test stimuli are converted to numerical data or numerically codeable data such as the scoring levels of the FSI-type interview. The scoring process can also be either "mechanical" or "human." In "mechanical" scoring, student responses are converted automatically, i.e. without any thought or judgment on the part of a human rater, to the appropriate score. This would include the scoring of multiple-choice responses, either by machine or by a human performing the same mechanical chore, and also the automatic evaluation of spoken responses through voice recognition devices or similar electronic means. In "human" scoring, one or more persons must actually listen to the responses of the examinee and exercise a certain degree of thought or judgment in arriving at a rating of the examinee's performance.

Test scoring, both mechanical and human, can be further divided into "simultaneous" scoring and "delayed" scoring. Simultaneous scoring is carried out on the spot, either during or immediately following the test itself, and there is no need to tape record or in any other way preserve the examinee's responses. In delayed scoring, the test responses of the examinee are recorded for evaluation at a later time.

Table 1 below summarizes possible combinations of administration technique (mechanical/human), scoring technique (mechanical/human), and time of scoring (simultaneous/delayed), and gives examples of actual tests or theoretically possible tests based on these combinations.

Table 1

An Inventory of Possible Administration and Scoring Modes for Oral Proficiency Testing

Administration	*Scoring*	*Time of Scoring*	*Examples*
1. Mechanical	Mechanical	Simul.	Speech Auto-Instructional Device (Buiten and Lane 1965); SCOPE Speech Interpreter (Pulliam 1969).
2. Mechanical	Mechanical	Delayed	As in (1), using previously recorded responses.
3. Mechanical	Human	Simul.	Test administration *via* tape recorder and/or visual stimuli; human scorer evaluates responses on-the-spot.
4. Mechanical	Human	Delayed	Tape recorded speaking tests in typical achievement batteries (*MLA-Cooperative Tests, MLA Proficiency Tests for Teachers and Advanced Students*).
5. Human	Mechanical	Simul.	Unlikely procedure.
6. Human	Mechanical	Delayed	Unlikely procedure.
7. Human	Human	Simul.	Face-to-face interviews (FSI; Peace Corps/ETS).
8. Human	Human	Delayed	As in (7), using previously recorded responses.

To discuss first the area of *direct* oral proficiency tests, the possible combinations of administration and scoring procedures are highly restricted by the need to provide a valid facsimile of the actual communicative situations. Since the instantaneous modification of topical content characteristic of real-life conversational situations cannot be duplicated through tape records or other mechanical means, "human" administration is required. This restricts the available possibilities to categories 5 through 8 in Table 1. Of these, human administration and mechanical scoring (categories 5 and 6) would involve the use of some type of device capable of analyzing complex conversational speech. At the present time, no such device is available.

The remaining categories are 7 and 8. Category 7—human administration and simultaneous human scoring—is exemplified by the face-to-face interview of the FSI type[1] in which one or more trained individuals administer the test stimuli (in the sense of holding a guided conversation with the examinee) and also evaluate the student's performance on a real-time basis. Category 8—human administration and delayed human scoring—would also involve a face-to-face conversation, but the scoring would be carried out at a later time using a tape recording of the interview or a videotape with a sound track.

From the standpoint of validity, tests in categories 7 and 8 approach real-life communication about as closely as is possible in the test situation. Face-to-face conversation between examiner and examinee on a variety of topics does, of course, differ to some extent from the contexts in which these communications take place in real life, and the psychological and affective components of the formal interview also differ somewhat from those of the real-life setting. As Perren points out: ". . . both participants know perfectly well that it is a test and not a tea-party, and both are subject to psychological tensions, and what is more important, to linguistic constraints of style and register thought appropriate to the occasion by both participants."[2] However, except, for such exotic and ultimately impractical techniques as surreptitiously observing the examinee in real-life linguistic settings—ordering meals, talking with friends, communicating on the job, and so forth—it is difficult to identify an oral proficiency measurement technique with a usefully higher level of face validity.

With respect to the *reliability* of the interview procedure, it can be asked whether simultaneous or delayed evaluation of the interview permits more reliable scoring. In connection with an interviewer training project which Educational Testing Service has been conducting with ACTION/Peace Corps, 80 FSI-type interviews in French were independently scored by two raters simultaneously present at the interview, and their ratings agreed as to basic score level (0, 1, 2, 3, 4, 5) in 95 percent of the cases. Scoring of tape recorded interviews by two or more independent raters (i.e. the "delayed" technique) has informally been observed to attain about the same levels of reliability, but much more detailed scoring reliability studies would be desirable for both modes of scoring.

Certain attributes of the simultaneous scoring procedure could be

---

[1]Rice 1959; Foreign Service Institute 1963.

[2]Perren 1967, p. 26.

viewed as more favorable to high scoring reliability than the delayed procedure. First, all relevant communicative stimuli are available to the scorer, including the examinee's facial expressions, gestures, lip movements, and so forth. Unless a video recording of the interview is made (rather than an ordinary tape recording), these components would be lost to the rater in the delayed scoring situation. Second, simultaneous scoring may benefit from a "recency of exposure" factor in that the rater has the conversation more clearly and more thoroughly in mind than he or any other scorer could have at a later time. Third, when the test administrator and scorer are present simultaneously (or when a single interviewer fills both roles), the interview can be lengthened or modified in certain ways which the scorer considers important to a comprehensive assessment of the candidate's performance. In delayed scoring, the rater must base his judgment on whatever is recorded on the tape, and he has no corrective recourse if the interview happens to be too brief or otherwise unsatisfactory for effective scoring. Finally, when the interview is scored on the spot, there is no possibility of encountering technical difficulties such as poorly recorded or otherwise distorted tapes that might hinder accurate scoring in the delayed situation.

On the other hand, there are a number of features of the delayed scoring arrangement that might be considered to enhance scoring reliability. First, there would be no opportunity for variables such as the interviewee's mannerisms or personal attractiveness to affect the scoring process. Second, there could be a better control on the scoring conditions, in that the interview tapes could be more effectively randomized, intermingled with tapes from other sources, and so forth than is usually the case when live examinees must be scheduled at a given testing site. Third, delayed scoring would allow for repetitive playback of all or selected portions of the interview to resolve points of doubt in the scorer's mind—a possibility which is not available in the simultaneous scoring situation.

In view of these and other conflicting interpretations of the potential reliabilities of simultaneous and delayed techniques, a comprehensive experimental study comparing these two procedures would seem very much in order.

With respect to the *practicality* of interview testing of the FSI type, an obvious concern is the need to involve expensive humans in both the test administration and scoring process. Since there appears to be no alternative to such an approach—at least within the context of direct proficiency testing—the question is reduced to that of making the most effective use of the human input required.

The manpower requirements can be reduced to a considerable extent by decreasing the total testing time per examinee. Interview tests of the FSI type typically require approximately 15 to 30 minutes, with somewhat shorter or longer testing times for very limited or extremely proficient examinees, respectively. Evaluation of the student's performance and assignment of a score level would usually require an additional 2 to 5 minutes beyond the running time of the interview itself. When interviewing on a group basis, it is difficult for a single tester or team of testers to administer more than about 15 interviews per day.

Since test administration time and the associated manpower expense is probably the largest single drawback to widespread use of the full-scale interview procedure, there would be considerable interest in determining the extent to which a face-to-face interview could be abbreviated without seriously affecting either the validity of the test or its scoring reliability. Considerable informal experience in connection with the Peace Corps testing project suggests that the examinee's basic score level (i.e. his assignment to one of the six verbally-defined score levels) can be fairly accurately established within the first 5 minutes of conversation. If evaluation at this level of specificity is considered acceptable—as distinguished from the detailed diagnostic information and assignment of applicable "plus" levels obtained in a full-length interview—test administration and scoring expense would be reduced by a factor of three or four.

Although shorter interview times do reduce the number of topical areas and styles of discourse that can be sampled, the effect on scoring reliability may not be so great as has commonly been assumed. In any event, the matter of optimum interview length is a strictly empirical question which should be thoroughly explored in a controlled experimental setting. An appropriate technique would be to have a large number of trained raters present at a given interview. At the end of fixed time intervals (such as every 5 minutes), subgroups of these raters would leave the interview room and assign ratings on the basis of the interview performance up to that time. These ratings would be checked for reliability against the ratings derived from partial interviews of other lengths and from the full-length "criterion" interview.

A second major component of interview practicality is the question of using 1 or 2 interviewers. The traditional FSI technique has been to use 2 trained interviewers wherever possible. One interviewer takes primary responsibility for leading the conversation, and the other carefully listens for and makes notes of areas of strength and weakness in the examinee's performance. The second interviewer may also intervene from time to time to steer the conversation into areas which the first interviewer may have overlooked. At the conclusion of the interview, both examiners discuss the student's performance and mutually determine the score level to be assigned. The chief disadvantage of the two-examiner technique is the increased manpower cost, which is effectively double that of the single-examiner procedure. Again, detailed comparative studies would be necessary to determine whether the participation of a second interviewer results in a substantial and economically-justifiable increase in scoring reliability.

In analyzing simultaneous and delayed interview *scoring* techniques from the standpoint of practicality, the simultaneous procedure appears clearly preferable. Indeed, simultaneous scoring can be considered almost "free of charge" in the sense that the examiner(s)—already necessarily on hand to administer the interview—require only a few additional moments to determine the appropriate score level. By contrast, delayed scoring requires the complete "replaying" of the interview, and although certain procedures such as time compression of the tape recording (Cartier 1968) or preliminary editing of several interviews into a single continuous tape (Rude 1967) might decrease the scoring time somewhat, it is doubtful that delayed scoring could ever be made as economical as simultaneous scoring carried out by the test administrators themselves. A further disadvantage of the delayed scoring technique is the appreciably longer turnaround time for score reports to students and instructors.

The preceding discussion of direct proficiency measurement techniques may be summarized as follows. The need to provide a face-valid communicative setting restricts test administration possibilities to the face-to-face interaction of a human tester and examinee. Because mechanical devices capable of evaluating speech in a conversational situation are not a viable possibility at the present time, the scoring of the test must also involve trained human participation. Within these constraints, the possibilities of selection among the eight testing categories shown are reduced to a choice between simultaneous and delayed scoring. The relative levels of reliability obtainable through simultaneous and delayed scoring have not been established on any rigorous basis, and logical arguments can be advanced in favor of both techniques. Considerations of practicality point to simultaneous scoring of the proficiency interview as an appreciably more efficient and economical technique.

Turning now to *indirect* measures of oral proficiency, the testing possibilities are expanded in that there is no longer a requirement for a face-valid (i.e. human-administered, conversational) administration setting, and mechanical administration techniques can be considered. With reference to Table 1, the first two categories of mechanical administration and mechanical scoring would involve such techniques as the student's imitation of isolated sounds or short phrases in the test language, with the responses evaluated by computer-based speech recognition devices. Buiten and Lane (1965) developed a Speech Auto-Instructional Device capable of extracting pitch, loudness, and rhythm parameters from short spoken phrases and comparing these to internally-stored criteria of accuracy. Pulliam (1969) has described the development of an experimental speech interpreter, also computer-based, which can evaluate the examinee's pronunciation of specific short utterances. Drawbacks to the use of these devices include equipment cost and complexity and also the extremely limited repertoire of sounds or phrases that can be evaluated with a single programming of the machines. It is also quite doubtful that even the very precise measurement of the student's pronunciation accuracy that might be afforded by these devices would show a high correlation with general proficiency, in view of the many other variables which are involved in the latter performance.

Category 3—mechanical test administration and simultaneous human scoring—does not appear to be productive. One possible application would be the tape recorded presentation of questions or other stimuli to which the examinee would respond, with on the spot evaluation by a human rater. Such a technique would, however, afford no saving in manpower over a regular face-to-face interview, and there would seem to be no practical reason to prefer it over the latter, more direct, technique as a means of overall proficiency testing.

Category 4—mechanical administration and delayed human scoring—offers considerably greater testing possibilities. Included in this category are the speaking tests in large-scale standardized batteries such as the *MLA Foreign Language Proficiency Tests for Teachers and Advanced Students* (Starr 1962); the *MLA-Cooperative Foreign Language Tests* (Educational Testing Service 1965); and the *Pimsleur Proficiency Tests* (Pimsleur 1967). The general technique in these and similar tests is to coordinate a master tape recording and student booklet in such a way that both aural stimuli (such as short phrases to be mimicked, questions to which the student responds) and visual stimuli (printed tests to be read aloud, pictures to be described, etc.) can be presented. The master tape also gives the test instructions and paces the student through the various parts of the test.

It is fairly well established that the types of speaking tasks presented in a standardized speaking test cannot be considered highly face-valid measures of the student's communicative proficiency. As previously indicated, the most serious drawback in this respect is that it is not possible to engineer a mechanically-administered test in such a way that the stimulus questions can be changed or modified on a real-time basis to correspond to the give-and-take of real-life communication. In addition to this basic difficulty, a substantial proportion of the specific testing formats used in these tests—mimicry of heard phrases, descriptions of pictures or series of pictures, reading aloud from a printed text—are at least some steps removed from the face-to-face conversational interaction implicit in the concept of oral proficiency. For these reasons, it appears more appropriate and more productive to classify and interpret the MLA Proficiency Tests, the MLA-Cooperative Tests, and similar instruments as *indirect* measures of oral proficiency which reveal their appropriateness as proficiency measures not through the observed validity of their setting, content, and operation but through the degree to which they may be found to correlate on a concurrent basis with direct measures of oral proficiency.

Unfortunately, the detailed correlational studies needed to establish the concurrent validity of these indirect measures *vis-a-vis* direct proficiency tests are for the most part lacking. In connection with a large-scale survey of the foreign language proficiency of graduating college language majors, Carroll (1967) administered both the speaking test from the MLA Proficiency Battery and the FSI interview test to small samples of students of French, German, Russian, and Spanish. Correlations ranging from .66 to .82 were obtained, representing moderate to good predictive accuracy. To the extent that scoring of the indirect speaking tests is itself an unreliable process, the observed correlations between these tests and the FSI interview or similar direct procedures would be attenuated.

It is interesting to note that standardized speaking tests of the MLA type are generally considered to have higher scoring reliabilities than the freer and less structured interview techniques. This opinion may be attributable in part to the impressive technical accouterments of the standardized tests, including the language laboratory administration setting and the accompanying master test tapes, student booklets, and response tapes. However, evidence available to date does not support a high level of scoring reliability for tests of this type.

Starr (1962) has discussed some of the difficulties encountered in the scoring of the MLA Proficiency Speaking Tests, including a "halo effect" when a single rater was required to score all sections of a given test tape and the gradual shifting of scoring standards in the course of the grading process. Scoring reliability of the MLA-Cooperative Speaking Tests was examined in a study of the two-rater scoring of 100 Fench test tapes (Educational Testing Service 1965). Among the different test sections, scoring reliability ranged from .78 (for the picture description section) to a low of .31 (mimicry of short phrases). The inter-rater reliability for the entire test was only .51. Scoring reliability for the Pimsleur speaking tests was not reported in the test manual, and Pimsleur indicated that "because of the nature of the test," the speaking test scores should be interpreted with caution.[3]

These results raise an interesting question—specifically, whether carefully designed direct proficiency interviews might not exceed in scoring reliability the levels so far observed for the more indirect standardized tests. Additional studies of the scoring reliabilities of both types of test would seem very much in order.

In regard to the question of *practicality*, mechanically-administered speaking tests do save administration time in that a number of students can be tested simultaneously in a language laboratory setting. However, during the scoring process each student response tape must still be evaluated individually by human listeners, and to the extent that the scoring time for the indirect recorded test approaches the combined administration/scoring time of the direct proficiency interview, any manpower advantage of the tape recorded procedure is lost.

With regard to typical scoring times for tape recorded tests, it is interesting to note that scorers evaluating the MLA Proficiency Test tapes on a volume basis were typically able to score approximately 15 tapes per day. It bears emphasizing that this rate is not appreciably different from the number of face-to-face interviews of the FSI type that a single individual can conveniently administer and score in a working day.

Widely varying scoring rates have been reported for other types of tape recorded speaking tests. These range from a maximum of about 1 hour per student to a minimum of about 5 minutes. The one-hour figure is reported by Davison and Geake (1970), who evaluated each student's responses according to a number of detailed criteria. The procedure also included frequent reference to external comparison tapes and considerable replaying of the student tapes. The five-minute scoring was accomplished by Beardsmore and Renkin (1971), using a shorter initial test and a tape recording technique which deleted from the student tapes all material other than the active responses.

Generally speaking, the scoring time for tape recorded tests is affected by a great number of factors, including the absolute length of the student's responses, the presence or absence of "dead" spaces in which test directions or stimuli are being heard instead of student responses, the frequency with which portions of the test must be replayed during scoring, the complexity of the scoring procedure itself, the amount of time required to mark down partial scores and calculate a total score, and even the rewind speed of the machines on

[3]Pimsleur 1967, p. 15

which the test tapes are played back. In the ideal situation, a combination of carefully planned test formats, technological aids such as voice-activated relays to operate the student recorders only during active responding, and concise and easily-applied scoring standards could reduce test scoring time considerably while providing for a sufficiently broad sampling of the student's speaking performance. On the other hand, lack of care in developing the test formats, administration procedures, and scoring techniques may well result in an indirect test of oral proficiency which is appreciably less cost-effective in terms of administration and scoring manpower than the direct proficiency interview itself.

All of the indirect tests discussed so far require active speech production on the student's part, even though the speaking tasks involved are not closely parallel to real-life communication activities. Although such tests may be felt to have a certain degree of face validity in the sense that the student is actually required to speak in a variety of stimulus situations, their true value as effective measures of communicative proficiency is more appropriately established on a concurrent validity basis, i.e. through statistical correlation with an FSI-type interview or other criterion test that is in itself highly face-valid. There is a second category of indirect tests in which the student is not even required to speak. Tests of this type must depend even more highly on correlational relationships with direct criterion tests to establish their validity as measures of oral proficiency.

Among these "non-speaking" speaking tests, the "reduced redundancy" technique developed by Bernard Spolsky is discussed at length elsewhere in this volume. Briefly, the reduced redundancy procedure involves giving the student a number of sentences in the target language which have been distorted by the introduction of white noise at various signal/noise levels. The student attempts to write out each sentence as it is heard. On the assumption that students who have a high degree of overall proficiency in the language can continue to understand the recorded sentences even when many of the redundant linguistic cues available in the undistorted sentence have been obliterated, the student's score on the test is considered indicative of his general level of language proficiency.

The Spolsky test has been validated against various listening comprehension, reading, and writing tests (Spolsky et al 1968; Spolsky 1971), with concurrent validity correlations ranging between .36 and .66. The reduced redundancy technique has not to the writer's knowledge been validated against the FSI interview or other tests requiring actual speech production on the student's part, and the extent of correlation of reduced redundancy tests with direct measures of speaking proficiency remains to be determined.

The "cloze" test is another indirect procedure which recently has received considerable attention. This technique, originated by W. L. Taylor (1953) in the context of native-language testing, involves the systematic deletion of letters or words from a continuous printed text, which the student is asked to resupply on the basis of contextual clues available in the remaining portion of the text. Numerous experimental studies of the cloze procedure have been carried out over the past several years (Carroll, Carton, and Wilds 1959; Oller and Conrad 1971), including investigations of the deletion of only certain categories of words such as prepositions (Oller and Inal 1971); computer-based scoring using a "clozentropy" formula based on information theory (Darnell 1968); and human scoring in which any contextually-acceptable response is considered correct, not necessarily the originally deleted word (Oller 1972).

Very satisfactory concurrent validity coefficients have been found for the cloze tests, using as criteria various other presumably more direct measures of overall language proficiency. Darnell (1968) reported a correlation of .84 between a 200-item cloze test and the total score on the Test of English as a Foreign Language (TOEFL). Oller (1972) obtained a correlation of .83 between a cloze test scored on a contextually-acceptable basis and the UCLA placement examination, consisting of vocabulary, grammar, reading, and dictation sections.

As is the case with reduced redundancy testing, there appears to be no experimental information currently available on the extent of correlation between cloze-type measures and direct tests of oral proficiency *per se;* such studies would be very useful in determining the extent to which tests based on the cloze procedure might be used as surrogates for direct oral proficiency testing.

In terms of practicality, both reduced redundancy tests and cloze procedures offer considerable advantages. Test administration can be carried out on a mechanical basis, using a test tape and student response booklet for the reduced redundancy test and a test booklet alone for the cloze procedure.

Scoring complexity and time required to score cloze tests depend on the particular grading system used. A major drawback of the Darnell clozentropy system is the need for computer-based computation in the course of the scoring process; this limits use of the clozentropy technique to schools or institutions having the necessary technical facilities. Human scoring of regular cloze tests is rapid and highly objective, especially when exact replacement of the original word is the scoring criterion. Multiple-choice versions of the cloze test are also possible, further speeding and objectifying the scoring process.

Despite the potentially high level of practicality of reduced redundancy and cloze techniques, the ultimate usefulness of these and other indirect techniques as measures of oral proficiency will rest on the magnitude of the correlations that can be developed between them and the more direct measures, correlations based on the simultaneous administration of both kinds of tests to examinee groups similar in personal characteristics and language learning history to those students who would eventually be taking only the indirect test. It should also be noted that tests which do not actually require the student to speak would probably not have as much motivational impact towards speaking practice and improvement as tests requiring oral production, especially the direct conversational interview. It may thus be desirable for pedagogical reasons to favor the direct testing of proficiency wherever possible.

This discussion may be concluded with a few summary remarks. If oral proficiency is defined as the student's ability to communicate accurately and effectively in real-life language-use contexts, especially in the face-to-face conversations typical of the great majority of real-world speech activities, considerations of face validity appear to require human administration of a conversation-based test, which must also be evaluated by human raters. For this reason, direct interview techniques deserve continuing close attention and experimental study aimed at improving both the test administration and scoring procedures. The latter must be continuously reviewed to insure that they call for examiner judgments of the student's communicative ability and effectiveness, rather than his command of specific linguistic features.[4] To permit practical and economical administration in the school setting, interview-based tests must also be designed to reach acceptable reliability levels within relatively short testing times.

Proponents of direct proficiency testing can be encouraged by the limited but tantalizing data which suggest that these techniques are competitive with current standardized speaking tests in terms of both scoring reliability and overall cost. The higher level of face validity of the direct proficiency techniques, together with the considerable motivational value inherent in work-sample tests of communicative ability, would commend these techniques to language teachers and testers alike for continuing investigation and increased practical use.

---

[4]On this point, see Clark 1972, pp. 121-129.

REFERENCES

Beardsmore, H. Baetens and A. Renkin (1971). "A Test of Spoken English." *International Review of Applied Linguistics* 9:1, 1-11.

Buiten, Roger and Harlan Lane (1965). "A Self-Instructional Device for Conditioning Accurate Prosody." *International Review of Applied Linguistics* 3:3, 205-219.

Carroll, John B. (1967). *The Foreign Language Attainments of Language Majors in the Senior Year: A Survey Conducted in U.S. Colleges and Universities.* Cambridge,

Mass.: Laboratory for Research in Instruction, Harvard University Graduate School of Education.

———, Aaron S. Carton, and Claudia P. Wilds (1959). *An Investigation of "Cloze" Items in the Measurement of Achievement in Foreign Languages.* Cambridge, Mass.: Laboratory for Research in Instruction, Harvard University Graduate School of Education.

Cartier, Francis A. (1968). "Criterion-Referenced Testing of Language Skills." *TESOL Quarterly* 2:1, 27-32.

Clark, John L. D. (1972). *Foreign Language Testing: Theory and Practice.* Philadelphia: Center for Curriculum Development.

Darnell, D. K. (1968). *The Development of an English Language Proficiency Test of Foreign Students Using a Clozentropy Procedure.* Boulder, Co.: Department of Speech and Drama, University of Colorado.

Davison, J. M. and G. M. Geake (1970). "An Assessment of Oral Testing Methods in Modern Languages." *Modern Languages* 51:3, 116-123.

Educational Testing Service (1965). *Handbook: MLA-Cooperative Foreign Language Tests.* Princeton, N.J.: Educational Testing Service.

Foreign Service Institute (1963). "Absolute Language Proficiency Ratings." (Circular.) Washington, D.C.: Foreign Service Institute.

Oller, John W., Jr. (1972). "Scoring Methods and Difficulty Levels for Cloze Tests of Proficiency in English as a Second Language." *Modern Languge Journal* 56:3, 151-158.

——— and Christine Conrad (1971). "The Cloze Technique and ESL Proficiency." *Language Learning* 21:2, 183-196.

——— and Nevin Inal (1971). "A Cloze Test of English Prepositions." *TESOL Quarterly* 5:4, 315-325.

Perren, George (1967). "Testing Ability in English as a Second Language: 3. Spoken Language." *English Language Teaching* 22:1, 22-29.

Pimsleur, Paul (1967). *Pimsleur French Proficiency Tests—Manual.* New York: Harcourt, Brace & World.

Pulliam, Robert (1969). *Application of the SCOPE Speech Interpreter in Experimental Educational Programs.* Fairfax, Va.: Pulliam and Associates.

Rice, Frank A. (1959). "The Foreign Service Institute Tests Language Proficiency." *Linguistic Reporter* 1:2, 4.

Rude, Ben D. (1967). "A Technique for Language Laboratory Testing." *Language Learning* 17:3 & 4, 151-153.

Spolsky, Bernard (1971). "Reduced Redundancy as a Language Testing Tool." In G. E. Perren and J. L. M. Trimm (eds.), *Applications of Linguistics: Selected Papers of the Second International Congress of Applied Linguistics, Cambridge, 1969.* Cambridge: Cambridge University Press, 383-390.

———, Bengt Sigurd, Masahito Sato, Edward Walker, and Catherine Arterburn (1968). "Preliminary Studies in the Development of Techniques for Testing Overall Second Language Proficiency." *Language Learning,* Special Issue No. 3, 79-101.

Starr, Wilmarth H. (1962). "MLA Foreign Language Proficiency Tests for Teachers and Advanced Students." *PMLA* 77:4, Part II, 1-12.

Taylor, Wilson L. (1953). "Cloze Procedure: A New Tool for Measuring Readability." *Journalism Quarterly* 30:4, 414-438.

DISCUSSION

Spolsky: There's one thing that might be worth thinking about that I think you excluded, and that is that the oral interview and so on comes out to be simply a conversation. There is also the possibility of considering the communication task as a test, the kind of situation where the examinee sits in a room, the telephone rings, he picks it up, somebody starts speaking to him in another language, and he has a choice of either using that language or trying to avoid using it. The other person is trying to get directions, and either he does get to the place he's supposed to or he doesn't. You can say at the end of the test that either he was capable of communicating or not. This kind of communication task test is one in which the judgment of its effectiveness is whether or not the speaker communicates with the listener. It would be theoretically possible to set this up in such a way that you have a mechanical rather than a human judgment. The problem of deciding what the qualities of the listening person need to be is one thing to be taken into account. But a person could be given mechanically a certain piece of information to communicate to a second person, the second person performs the task, and if he performs it successfully, then mechanically this could be scored in such a way. From the results of previous experiments, there appears to be a way of testing communication ability, which is the speaking side, that has absolutely no correlation with other indirect measures of language ability. I wonder if you'd perhaps like to comment on that?

Clark: I'm fairly familiar with that and similar techniques. I'd say certainly any and all testing techniques we can devise or think of merit consideration. The question would be whether we'd be willing to call this kind of thing a face valid direct test of proficiency. My own inclination would be to stick with the real conversational situation as the criterion test, and then hope that we could develop a correlation of .99 or thereabouts between the face-to-face interview and some other kind of measure.

Lado: I don't think there is any merit in face validity; face validity means the appearance of validity. I think that there are questions concerning the interview from the point of view of sample, and I think that the interview is a poor sample. For example, most interviews don't give the subject a chance to ask questions. He gets asked questions, but he doesn't ask them. And it seems to me that asking questions is a very important element of communication. Second, the interview will usually go on to some limited number of topics. Who is able to produce 100 different original topics of conversation with 100 different subjects? Therefore, it may not even be a very good sample of situations. So I think that the question of the validity of the sample itself isn't proven. Then, it's been mentioned by everybody that the interview is highly subjective. There is what can be termed a "halo effect." I'd hate to be interviewed after somebody who's terrific, because no matter what I am, I'm going to be cut down. I'd like to come after somebody who got a rating of 0+, then my chances of showing up are better. There's the personality of the interviewer and interviewee. There's also the fact of accents. Sociolinguistics has shown that we react differently to different accents. For example, the Spanish accent in an English-speaking test will tend to rate lower than a French or a German accent, or some other accent like that. There is also the problem of keeping the level of scoring more or less even. It's true that you can record these interviews and go back to them, but it's more likely that there will be some drifting away or raising of standards as you go. I think the scoring of nine or ten or eleven points is coarse. It's a mixed bag, and it's all right perhaps for certain purposes, but if we have to use this interview six years in a row in a language sequence, we would find that a lot of students would remain at 1 for five years. We might conclude that they haven't learned anything, but I think there might be finer ways of finding out if they have learned something, if in fact they have. I think that the interview is a poor test of listening. And I certainly go along with the CIA on this—they have a separate listening test. How many questions do you ask an interviewee? I'm sure the reliability of the listening part would be very poor. Finally, I think the interview mixes skills with proficiency, and I think Clark is on the right track in his book when he says you can't do both of them in one interview. You're either after proficiency, and don't get down to the specifics, or you get down to the competence, and there are better ways to do this than the interview. I am in disagreement with Clark's pejorative intimation concerning indirect techniques, and his favorable "halo" toward direct techniques.

Clark: Let's discuss that later.

Anon.: How long does it take to train a tester?

Clark: Our Peace Corps experience might be helfpul in answering that question. We think that we're able to train a tester in 2 days of face-to-face work and discussion, preceded by a couple of days of homework on his part—reading an instructional manual, listening to sample tapes and so forth. I'd suggest that this kind of time requirement is pretty much in line with the amount of time it takes to train someone to score the MLA COOP tests, for example. So I think we can be cost-effective in terms of the training time of the interviewer.

Anon.: As I understood the FSI technique, 95 percent of the raters agreed in the rating that was given. Is that correct?

Clark: First let me say that it was a fairly small-scaled study. Some 80 interviews were examined. We need a much more comprehensive study of this. But of those 80 interviews, two raters were simultaneously present during the interview. Then at the end of the interview they independently rated on the basis of 1 2 3 4 5, not 1+ vs. 2, for example. But within the categories 1 2 3 4 5, 95 percent of their ratings were identical.

Anon.: Isn't it odd that there were correlations of .31 in the other types of tests that were given?

Clark: Yes, I think that's very interesting. I hoped that that would come across.

Scott: I question whether a one-shot test is really adequate.

Clark: If you are talking about determining a student's proficiency at a specific point in time, rather than determining any sort of growth that he makes, I would say that a one-shot test is sufficient, provided that the test is a valid and reliable representation of his ability. If we find that within the space of 2 or 3 days he's administered the test five times and he gets widely varying scores, then our test is in trouble. But if we have a test which can reliably evaluate on a "single shot" basis, all the better.

Spolsky: May I just make one brief comment on that? As I remember we talked about this problem a couple of years ago, that's the problem that proficiency tests are also used as predictors of how people will perform when put into a new language environment. The question was raised then that, while you may have two people at exactly the same point on the proficiency scale, you do want to know which of them, when thrown completely into the language speaking situation, will learn faster, and I think that's a fairly strong argument for a two-shot test or a kind of test that will also find out at what point on the language learning continuum the learner happens to be.

Oller: I'd like to make three quick comments. I want to agree very strongly with what John Clark said about the oral interview and the reasons why he thinks that's a realistic kind of thing to demand of people. Unfortunately, natural situations sometimes generate tension, and I don't think that's an argument against the oral interview. The second comment is that it seems to me that there's another kind of validity that correlational validity is in evidence for. And I would suggest a term something like psycholinguistic validity. It's something that has to do with what is, in fact, in a person's brain that enables him to operate with language. And if we're tapping into that fundamental mechanism, then I think we have a deeper kind of validity than face validity or correlational validity or some of the others. Correlational validity is, I think, evidence of that kind of deeper validity. The third comment is that, in reference to the low correlation on the mimicry test, I think that that's very possibly due to the fact that short phrases were used. If longer phrases were used that challenged the short-term memory of the person being interviewed and forced him to operate on the basis of his deep, underlying system or grammar, I think the test would yield much higher validity.

Clark: Perhaps the .31 correlation for mimicry could be increased, as you suggest, by having longer sentences or something similar. But I think the general point is still valid that, if you look at the test manuals or handbooks for these tests—the Pimsleur Test manual, for example—you'll find no reliability figures for the scoring of the speaking test, and you'll find a caution to the effect that the score ranges must be interpreted very carefully, or words to this effect. If you look at the MLA COOP handbook, you will find reasonably low correlation figures and also cautions against misinterpretation and so forth. So I think that, as a general principle, the "high correlations" of tape recorded speaking tests are more fiction than fact.

Davies: Can I make two or three quick comments? First of all, following up some of the points made about validity, Mr. Clark distinguishes face validity and concurrent validity and relates these to his indirect and direct methods. I'd like to see content validity mentioned as well. I think in a way this is what is behind some of Professor Lado's remarks. If content validity is used, would you then be engaged in direct or indirect testing? And, would the psycholinguistic thing we just mentioned be considered construct validity? Finally, I'd like to comment on the question about the one-shot proficiency testing. It seems to me to be a function of the reliability of the test.

Clark: To take the last comment first, I think we are together on the question of the one-shot test. I said if the test is a reliable indication of ability in the sense that it can be repeated with the same score, why give all the different tests rather than the one? I think the question of construct validity or psycholinguistic validity, however we want to talk about it, will be coming up again. Regarding the first question, content validity vs. face validity, I may have given a slightly wrong impression about what I think face validity involves. Face validity for me would be careful examination by people who know their stuff: language people and language testers look at the test, at what it's got in it, at the way it's administered, at the way it's scored, in other words they look at the whole business of it, and this is face validity in my sense, as opposed to a statistical correlation validity. True, we don't want to rule out very close scrutiny of the test, and I think we'll keep that under the term face validity.

The Oral Interview Test

Claudia P. Wilds

Since 1956 the Foreign Service Institute of the Department of State has been rating Government employees on a simple numerical scale which succinctly describes speaking proficiency in a foreign language. This scale has become so widely known and well understood that a reference to a point on the scale is immediately and accurately intelligible to most people concerned with personnel assignments in the numerous Government foreign affairs agencies who now use the FSI rating system.

The usefulness of the system is based on careful and detailed definition, in both linguistic and functional terms, of each point on the scale.

This paper is concerned, first, with a description of the testing procedures and evaluation techniques whereby the rating system is currently applied at the Foreign Service Institute and the Central Intelligence Agency and, second, with the problems that seem to be inherent in the system.

BACKGROUND

Prior to 1952 there was no inventory of the language skills of Foreign Service Officers and, indeed, no device for assessing such skills. In that year, however, a new awareness of the need for such information led to preliminary descriptions of levels of proficiency and experimental rating procedures. By 1956 the present rating system and testing methods had been developed to a practicable degree.

Both the scope and the restrictions of the testing situation provided problems and requirements previously unknown in language testing. The range of these unique features is indicated below:

- The need to assess both speaking and reading proficiency within a half-hour to an hour. The requirement was imposed principally by the limited time available in the examinee's crowded schedule.
- The need to measure the complete range of language competence, from the skill acquired in 100 hours of training or a month of experience abroad to the native facility of someone who received his entire education through the foreign language.
- A population consisting of all the kinds of Americans serving the United States overseas: diplomats at all stages of their careers, secre-

taries, agricultural specialists, Peace Corps volunteers, soldiers, tax experts, and many others. They might have learned their language skills at home, on the job, or through formal training, in any combination and to any degree. Generally no biographical information was available beforehand.

- The necessity for a rating system applicable to any language; easy to interpret by examiners, examinees, and supervisors; and immediately useful in decisions about assignments, promotions, and job requirements.
- The need for unquestioned face validity and reputation of high reliability among those who take the test and those who use the results.

With these restrictions there was, from the beginning, very little choice in the kind of test that could be given. A structured interview custom-built to fit each examinee's experience and capabilities in the language promised to use the time allowed for the test with maximum efficiency. A rating scale, with units gross enough to ensure reasonable reliability, was developed on the basis of both linguistic and functional analyses. The definitions, which appear at the end of this article, are a modified version worked out by representatives of FSI, the CIA, and the Defense Language Institute in 1968 to fit the characteristics of as broad a population of Government employees as possible.

PROCEDURE

The testing team at FSI consists of a native speaker of the language being tested and a certified language examiner who may be either an experienced native-speaking language instructor or a linguist thoroughly familiar with the language. At the CIA two native speakers who are language instructors conduct the test.

The usual speaking test at FSI is conducted by the junior member of the testing team, who is always a native speaker. The senior member, who normally has native or near-native English, observes and takes notes. To the greatest extent possible the interview appears as a relaxed, normal conversation in which the senior tester is a mostly silent but interested participant. At the CIA the two interviewers take turns participating and observing. The procedures to be described here are primarily those which are used at FSI, which can normally take advantage of having one examiner who is a native speaker of English.

The test begins with simple social formulae in the language being tested: introductions, comments on the weather, questions like, "Have you just come back from overseas?", or "Is this the first time you've taken a test here?"

The examinee's success in responding to these opening remarks will determine the course of the rest of the test. If he fails to understand some of them, even with repetition and rephrasing, or does not answer easily, at least a preliminary ceiling is put on the level of questions to be asked. He will be asked as simply as possible to talk about himself, his family, and his work; he may be asked to give street directions, to play a role (e.g. renting a house), or to act as interpreter for the senior tester on a tourist level. Rarely, he may handle these kinds of problems well enough to be led on to discussions of current events or of detailed aspects of his job. Usually he is clearly pegged at some point below the S-2 rating.

The examinee who copes adequately with the preliminaries generally is led into natural conversation on autobiographical and professional topics. The experienced interviewer will simultaneously attempt to elicit the grammatical features that need to be checked. As the questions increase in complexity and detail, the examinee's limitations in vocabulary, structure, and comprehension normally become apparent quite rapidly. (A competent team usually can narrow the examinee's grade to one of two ratings within the first five or ten minutes; they spend the rest of the interview collecting data to verify their preliminary conclusions and to make a final decision.)

If the examinee successfully avoids certain grammatical features, if the opportunity for him to use them does not arise, or if his comprehension or fluency is difficult to assess, the examiners may use an informal interpreting situation appropriate to the examinee's apparent level of proficiency. If the situation is brief and plausible and the interchange yields a sufficient amount of linguistic information, this technique is a valuable supplement.

A third element of the speaking test, again an optional one, involves instructions or messages which are written in English and given to the examinee to be conveyed to the native speaker (e.g. "Tell your landlord that the ceiling in the living room is cracked and leaking and the sofa and rug are ruined.") This kind of task is particularly useful for examinees who are highly proficient on more formal topics or who indicate a linguistic self-confidence that needs to be challenged.

In all aspects of the interview an attempt is made to probe the examinee's functional competence in the language and to make him aware of both his capacities and limitations.

The speaking test ends when both examiners are satisfied that they have pinpointed the appropriate S-rating, usually within a half hour or less.

EVALUATION

When the interview is over, the examiners at FSI independently fill out the "Checklist of Performance Factors" with which they are provided. This checklist, reproduced at the end of this article, records a profile of the examinee's relative strengths and weaknesses, but was designed principally to force each examiner to consider the five elements involved.

A weighted scoring system for the checklist has been derived from a multiple correlation with the overall S-rating assigned (R=.95). The weights are basically these: Accent 0, Grammar 3, Vocabulary 2, Fluency 1, Comprehension 2. Partly because the original data came mainly from tests in Indo-European languages and partly because of a widespread initial suspicion of statistics among the staff, use of the scoring system has never been made compulsory or even urged, though the examiners are required to complete the checklist. The result has been that most examiners compute the checklist score only in cases of doubt or disagreement. Nevertheless, the occasional verifications of the checklist profiles seem to keep examiners in all languages in line with each other (in the sense that an S-2 in Japanese will have much the same profile as an S-2 in Swahili); and those who once distrusted the system now have faith in it.

To the trained examiner each blank on each scale indicates a quite specific pattern of behavior. The first two scales, Accent and Grammar, obviously indicate features that can be described most concretely for each language. The last three refer to features that are easy to equate from language to language but difficult to describe except in functional terms and probably dangerous to measure from so small a sample of speech on a scale more refined than these six-point ones.

The checklist does not apply to S-0s or S-5s and thus reflects the nine ratings from S-0+ to S-4+. Since each of the checklist factors is represented on a scale with only six segments, a check placed on a particular scale indicates a degree of competence not necessarily tied to a specific S-rating. The mark for Grammar for an S-3, for example, may fall anywhere from the third to the fifth segment, while an S-3's comprehension is typically in the fifth or sixth segment. In any case, the examiner is prevented from putting down an unconsidered column of checks to denote a single S-rating.

The rating each examiner gives is normally not based on the checklist, however, but on a careful interpretation of the amplified definitions of the S-ratings. It might be said here that successful interpretation depends not only on the perceptiveness of the examiner but at least as much on the thoroughness of his training and the degree to which he accepts the traditional meaning of every part of each definition.

The actual determination of the S-rating is handled differently from team to team at FSI. In some cases the two examiners vote on paper, in others one suggests a grade and the other agrees or disagrees and gives his reasons for dissent. In some a preliminary vote is taken, and disagreement leads to further oral testing until accord is reached. If a half-point discrepancy cannot be resolved by discussion or averaging of the computed scores from the checklist, the general rule followed at FSI is that the lower rating is given. (The rationale for this rule is that the rating is a promise of performance made by FSI to assignment officers and future supervisors. The consequences of overrating are more serious than the consequences of underrating, however disappointing the marginal decision may be to the examinee himself.)

At the CIA each examiner, without discussion, independently makes a mark on a segmented five-inch line whose polar points are 0 and 5. The distance from 0 to the mark is later measured with a ruler and the two lengths are averaged for the final rating. CIA testers tend less to analyze the examinee's performance in detail; functional effectiveness is the overriding criterion.

PROBLEMS

To those who have little or no familiarity with the rating system just described, there may be a dozen reasons that come to mind why it should not work well enough to be a practical and equitable procedure. Most of the troublesome elements have by now been removed or made tolerable by the necessity for facing them repeatedly. The articulate anger of a Foreign Service Officer who feels his career threatened by a low rating is enough to make those who give such a rating aware that they must be able to defend it, and the occasional but vigorous complaints, especially in the early years, have done much to shape and refine the procedures.

One issue, for example, which has been resolved at the cost of many challenges is the question of acceptance by the examiners of social dialects which are not accepted by most educated native speakers of the language. Although many employees of the foreign aid program and perhaps a majority of Peace Corps volunteers work with illiterate and semi-literate people, it was decided that making non-standard speech and standard speech equally acceptable would make a shambles of the system, in large part because foreign speakers' errors are often identical with the patterns of uneducated native speakers. By insisting on the criteria developed for the speech of Foreign Service Officers, who obviously must speak the standard dialect, we avoided having to evolve several sets of rating definitions for other Government agencies.

The problems that are inherent in the system do *not* include reliability among raters of the same performance. Independent judgments on taped tests rarely vary more than a half-point (that is, a *plus*) from the assigned rating. A more serious issue is the stability of performance with different sets of interviewers. Because this kind of testing is so expensive, immediate retesting is not permitted, especially if it is only for research purposes. Consequently, there are two legitimate and interesting questions that FSI cannot answer: (1) Does the proficiency of the speaker of a foreign language fluctuate measurably from day to day? (2) Does his performance vary with the competence and efficiency of the examiners?

Individualizing the content of each interview has always seemed the best way to make optimum use of the time available. But this freedom that the interviewers have allows for the development of several kinds of inefficiency. The most common is the failure to push the more proficient examinee to the limits of his linguistic competence, so that data are lacking to make a reasonable decision between two grades. Often the intellectual ability to discuss a difficult topic may be confused with linguistic ability, although the structures and vocabulary used may be relatively simple ones. Another danger is the possibility, especially when both interviewers are native speakers of the language being tested, that both will participate so actively in the conversation that, for one thing, the examinee gets little chance to talk, and, for another, neither examiner keeps track of the kinds of errors being made or the types of structures that have not been elicited. The interview is designed to be as painless as possible, but it is not a social occasion, and the rating assigned can only be defended if it is based on a detailed analysis of the examinee's performance as well as on a general impression. For this same reason one examiner testing alone is likely to lose both his skills as an interviewer and his perceptiveness as an observer to a degree that cannot be justified on the grounds of economy.

There is thus a continuing possibility that the examinee may not be given the opportunity to provide a fully adequate sample of his speech and that the sample he does provide is not inspected with adequate attention. The obvious way to minimize the chances of this happening is through a rigorous training period for new examiners; intermittent programs of restandardizing; and, where possible, shuffling members of a testing team with great frequency.

The training of testers at FSI has improved greatly in recent years, largely because of the task that the staff had for several years of testing vast numbers of Peace Corps volunteers and then teaching others how to do so. In languages which are tested often there are good libraries of tapes of tests at all levels which the new interviewer can use to learn first the rating system and then the testing techniques before he puts them into practice in the testing room. There is also a substantial amount of written material aimed at clarifying standards and suggesting appropriate techniques, as well as a staff that now has years of experience in guiding others in testing competence.

Difficulties arise chiefly in languages that are tested so rarely that it is hard for the interviewers to internalize standards or to develop facility in conducting interviews at levels appropriate to different degrees of proficiency. In a number of languages the majority of tests are given in a week's time several times a year to graduating students whom the examiners know well and whose range of proficiency is relatively narrow. The rest of the tests in that language may number no more than a half dozen scattered throughout the year, at unpredictable levels of competence. It is too often the case that the native speaker interviewing in such a language knows no other language that is tested with more frequency, and it has been true more than once that the senior tester involved is equally restricted. At the same time, no one else on the staff may be familiar with the language involved. When this happens, the testers of that language cannot be adequately trained, tests cannot be effectively monitored, and both standards and procedures may diverge from the norm. In such cases one can only have faith in the clarity of the guidelines and the intelligence and conscientiousness of the examiners. (One form of control could be a periodic analysis of recorded tests by a highly qualified tester of another language who would go over the tapes line by line with the original interviewers.)

Even in languages in which tests are conducted as frequently as French and Spanish, where there is no doubt that standards are internalized and elicitation techniques are mastered, it is possible for criteria to be tightened or relaxed unwittingly over a period of several years so that ratings in the two languages are not equivalent or that current ratings are discrepant from those of earlier years.

The fact of the matter is that this system works. Those who are subject to it and who use the results find that the ratings are valid, dependable, and therefore extremely useful in making decisions about job assignments. It is, however, very much an in-house system which depends heavily on having all interviewers under one roof, able to consult with each other and share training advances in techniques or solutions to problems of testing as they are developed and subject to periodic monitoring. It is most apt to break down as a system when examiners are isolated by spending long periods away from home base (say a two-year overseas assignment), by testing in a language no one else knows, or by testing so infrequently or so independently that they evolve their own system.

It is therefore not ideal for the normal academic situation where all testing comes at once (making it difficult to acquire facility in interviewing ahead of time) and where using two teachers to test each student would be prohibitively expensive. It can be and has been applied in high schools and colleges where the ratings are not used as end-of-course grades but as information about the effectiveness of the teaching program or as a way of discovering each student's ability to use the language he has been studying.

FSI Language Proficiency Ratings

The rating scales described below have been developed by the Foreign Service Institute to provide a meaningful method of characterizing the language skills of foreign service personnel of the Department of State and of other Government agencies. Unlike academic grades, which measure achievement in mastering the content of a prescribed course, the S-rating for speaking proficiency and the R-rating for reading proficiency are based on the absolute criterion of the command of an educated native speaker of the language.

The definition of each proficiency level has been worded so as to be applicable to every language; obviously the amount of time and training required to reach a certain level will vary widely from language to language, as will the specific linguistic features. Nevertheless, a person with S-3s in both French and Chinese, for example, should have approximately equal linguistic competence in the two languages.

The scales are intended to apply principally to Government personnel engaged in international affairs, especially of a diplomatic, political, economic and cultural nature. For this reason heavy stress is laid at the upper levels on accuracy of structure and precision of vocabulary sufficient to be both acceptable and effective in dealings with the educated citizen of the foreign country.

As currently used, all the ratings except the S-5 and R-5 may be modified by a plus (+), indicating that proficiency substantially exceeds the minimum requirements for the level involved but falls short of those for the next higher level.

DEFINITIONS OF ABSOLUTE RATINGS

Elementary Proficiency

S-1 *Able to satisfy routine travel needs and minimum courtesy requirements.* Can ask and answer questions on topics very familiar to him; within the scope of his very limited language experience can understand simple questions and statements, allowing for slowed speech, repetition or paraphrase; speaking vocabulary inadequate to express anything but the most elementary needs; errors in pronunciation and grammar are frequent, but can be understood by a native speaker used to dealing with foreigners attempting to speak his language; while topics which are "very familiar" and elementary needs vary considerably from individual to individual, any person at the S-1 level should be able to order a simple meal, ask for shelter or lodging, ask and give simple directions, make purchases, and tell time.

R-1 *Able to read some personal and place names, street signs, office and shop designations, numbers, and isolated words and phrases.* Can recognize all the letters in the printed version of an alphabetic system and high-frequency elements of a syllabary or a character system.

Limited Working Proficiency

S-2 *Able to satisfy routine social demands and limited work requirements.* Can handle with confidence but not with facility most social situations including introductions and casual conversations about current events, as well as work, family, and autobiographical information; can handle limited work requirements, needing help in handling any complications or difficulties; can get the gist of most conversations on non-technical subjects (i.e. topics which require no specialized knowledge) and has a speaking vocabulary sufficient to express himself simply with some circumlocutions; accent, though often quite faulty, is intelligible; can usually handle elementary constructions quite accurately but does not have thorough or confident control of the grammar.

R-2 *Able to read simple prose, in a form equivalent to typescript or printing, on subjects within a familiar context.* With extensive use of a dictionary can get the general sense of routine business letters, international news items, or articles in technical fields within his competence.

Minimum Professional Proficiency

S-3 *Able to speak the language with sufficient structural accuracy and vocabulary to participate effectively in most formal and informal conversations on practical, social, and professional topics.* Can discuss particular interests and special fields of competence with reasonable ease; comprehension is quite complete for a normal rate of speech; vocabulary is broad enough that he rarely has to grope for a word; accent may be obviously foreign; control of grammar good; errors never interfere with understanding and rarely disturb the native speaker.

R-3 *Able to read standard newspaper items addressed to the general reader, routine correspondence, reports and technical material in his special field.* Can grasp the essentials of articles of the above types without using a dictionary; for accurate understanding moderately frequent use of a dictionary is required. Has occasional difficulty with unusually complex structures and low-frequency idioms.

Full Professional Proficiency

S-4 *Able to use the language fluently and accurately on all levels normally pertinent to professional needs.* Can understand and participate in any conversation within the range of his experience with a high degree of fluency and precision of vocabulary; would rarely be taken for a native speaker, but can respond appropriately even in unfamiliar situations; errors of pronunciation and grammar quite rare; can handle informal interpreting from and into the language.

R-4 *Able to read all styles and forms of the language pertinent to professional needs.* With occasional use of a dictionary can read moderately difficult prose readily in any area directed to the general reader, and all material in his special field including official and professional documents and correspondence; can read reasonably legible handwriting without difficulty.

Native or Bilingual Proficiency

S-5 *Speaking proficiency equivalent to that of an educated native speaker.* Has complete fluency in the language such that his speech on all levels is fully accepted by educated native speakers in all of its features, including breadth of vocabulary and idiom, colloquialisms, and pertinent cultural references.

R-5 *Reading proficiency equivalent to that of an educated native.* Can read extremely difficult and abstract prose, as well as highly colloquial writings and the classic literary forms of the language. With varying degrees of difficulty can read all normal kinds of handwritten documents.

Checklist of Performance Factors

1. ACCENT	foreign	__: __ __: __ __: __	native
2. GRAMMAR	inaccurate	__: __ __: __ __: __	accurate
3. VOCABULARY	inadequate	__: __ __: __ __: __	adequate
4. FLUENCY	uneven	__: __ __: __ __: __	even
5. COMPREHENSION	incomplete	__: __ __: __ __: __	complete

DISCUSSION

Nickel: I'm particularly interested in evaluations. In connection with this, was there any particular reason for weighting grammar with 3 points over 2 points on the vocabulary side?

Wilds: It was decided statistically. We had some 800 people fill out the checklist, then correlated it with the overall S-rating they assigned.

Nickel: Has there been any attempt to arrange these factors in hierarchical order, with preference given to the vocabulary side or to the grammatical side?
Wilds: According to the weights I think grammar is considered the most important of the five.
Nickel: Is there a linguistic basis for this?
Wilds: No.
Petersen: You encourage people to ignore accent?
Wilds: The fact is that they essentially do ignore it once the speaker is intelligible.
Jones: Could I just say concerning language testing, or any testing for that matter, there is in addition to face validity the initial reaction on the part of the person looking at this type of test? Almost without exception all the people I know who have seen or heard about an oral interview test for the first time react with shock. It can't be done. It's too subjective. There's no way to evaluate it. This was my reaction too when I was first exposed to it. But after having observed or participated in more than 100 oral interview tests, I find that it's a very valid system. First of all, in the training of the testers we don't only use these definitions that have been passed out to you today. These are only for the consumer, to indicate roughly what the levels are supposed to be. New testers have to be told in great detail what is to be expected on the part of the examinee in terms of content as well as the structure of the language. After the training period, they do have a pretty good intuitive idea of what a 2-level speaker is supposed to be able to do. We are in the process now of doing a validity study—a cross-agency study in three different languages—and we are finding that the reliability is very good. In other words, the tester does have a good idea of what the various levels are supposed to be in terms of performance. As far as fright is concerned, in observing many tests I have found that it does occur, but primarily only initially. A good tester can set the stage to be able to minimize this shock. I might add that many of us have looked around and have found nothing suitable for our purposes to take the place of the oral interview test. It has to be a test which, as much as possible, can recreate the situation the person is going to be exposed to when he has to use the language. I'd like to ask John Quiñones to explain the scale and use of the ruler at the CIA, and about the independent rating system.
Quiñones: When I first had to deal with testing at the Central Intelligence Agency, I found that the two testers would consult with each other, and if they differed, they would write the rating down on a piece of paper, discuss it further, and then decide which rating they were going to assign the individual. I thought this wasn't a very good idea, because one tester might tend to be a bit more dominant than the other, or one might have more experience than the other. I was afraid that in many instances one rater, in spite of the fact that he might have the wrong rating, would be the dominant rater. In order to avoid this, we developed a system in which raters would rate inde-

pendently using a scale with defined levels. Instead of discrete items on a given scale, they were defined as ranges. The testers, without discussing anything whatsoever, would indicate by writing within a given range, let's say the range of the 2 or the range of the 3, a line indicating how high or how low the person was in that range. Then, without any discussion, these sheets would be taken to a scorer, who, using a ruler divided into centimeters, would then measure each rating, average them, and arrive at a final rating. If a discrepancy existed by more than a level and a half, we would look for a third rater. After some studies we concluded that this is probably one of the most accurate, and one of the best, ways of assuring the reliability of the score, because we know that statistically the average rating is always more accurate than the rating of the best scorer.

Oller: I don't see any basis for that kind of detailed analysis without some fairly solid research to show that it's superior. All you're doing is multiplying the points on the scale. To get back to the discussion at hand, however, it seems to me that the system of oral interview can work. I feel that it would be possible to operationalize the definitions of what constitutes a zero rating, or a five rating by simply making some permanent recordings and keeping them in store, using them in the training of interviewers and in testing the reliability of different groups of interviewers against a collection of data based on that store of tapes. If that kind of calibration is done, and if reliability research indicates that interviewers are capable of agreeing on that particular set of tapes, then I think that you've got some pretty solid evidence that the interview is working.

Wilds: That works in the case of the more commonly tested languages, but it just isn't available for languages where fewer than 30 tests are given a year, which may reflect only six levels of proficiency.

Spolsky: I think that the question that Professor Lado raised earlier about the validity of an interview is a very good one, because one can ask whether or not an interview is valid for more than performance in an interview. That is, to what extent does performance in an interview predict performance in other kinds of real-life situations. From a sociolinguistic viewpoint, one can define a whole group of situations in which people are expected to perform—interacting with different kinds of subjects, speaking to different kinds of people about different kinds of topics. The question can be raised to what extent an interview and a conversation can sample all of these situations. I raised that question before, when talking about the work Tucker has done, where he has defined specific communication situations. Perhaps I could raise it again from this question. To what extent have there been studies of the accuracy of judgments made on the basis of FSI interviews? To what extent is there follow-up work, to what extent is there feed-back, when examinees go out into a real-world situation? Is there any way of finding out how accurately these judgments work out?

Wilds: This has not been systematically examined as far as I know. Certainly not recently. When we used to have regional language supervisors visiting embassies overseas, there were checks of sorts. Mostly the feed-back has been silence. Occasionally supervisors have said, "You've been unjust and should have given a higher rating to someone that you've underrated." But there hasn't been a systematic study made, for example, by following someone around all day in his job.

Spolsky: In other words, what you'd get would be complaints, and these complaints would depend presumably on whether a language-essential job is in fact a language-essential job. If somebody who has been rated on one of these things could move into what is described as a language-essential job, but is not required to use it a great deal, there would be no complaint.

Frey: I'm wondering if the oral interview is an effective way of testing grammar and vocabulary. Can't we do a better job by paper and pencil tests?

Wilds: If you want that kind of separate information. The question is whether it would supply information that is useful to people as far as proficiency on the job goes or as far as going into training.

Frey: Are you testing some other type of vocabulary and grammar, then? I always thought that there was just one type of grammar and vocabulary. I notice you have given grammar a weighting of 3 and vocabulary a weighting of 2. That's a very high weighting for the oral interview. And if one comes out very high in these, does that mean he can communicate? Someone can communicate very well while still having many grammatical errors in his speech.

Wilds: But if you can't put words together and don't have any vocabulary to put together, you can't communicate.

Oller: Along that line, do you know what the correlation is between the different scales? I frankly don't believe the difference between grammar and vocabulary on tests. I would expect those to be very highly intercorrelated.

Wilds: I think they are. I'd like to reiterate that the checklist does not normally determine the grade. It's supportive evidence, and it's relatively rarely calculated. It simply provides the testing unit with a profile. Usually at FSI the examiner takes notes on the performance and will report to the examinee, if he is interested, where his weaknesses are. But it's not the determining factor.

Davies: Could I ask a different sort of question which relates to your comment about the acceptance of social dialects? It seems to me very sensible. I wonder whether you have any experience with dialects of a different nature, for example, geographical dialects; whether you have the same attitude toward them, or how you handle what we might call "age-related" dialects, in the sense of how young people now speak?

Wilds: Except at the highest levels of the scale, this probably is not important. Somebody who is up through a 3+ is not likely to make that a problem for the examiner. He would look more like other 3's or 2+'s than he would like the native speaker of a particular age group.

Cartier: Following up on a couple of things that Professor Spolsky said a moment ago. First of all, what Spolsky wants to do that we're not doing is to make a distinction between whether language is the problem or whether language is the solution to a problem. Being a communication man rather than a linguist, I tend to side with Spolsky on this. The problem is communication, the solution is language, or a partial solution is language. And what Spolsky wants to do is to assure that the measures that we make, whereby we're going to predict the operational capability of a man on the job, are concerned with his ability to communicate and cope with real-life behaviors, regardless of whether he is linguistically qualified. And let me point out that without at least metric access to the criterion situation, we have what we must call a surrogate criterion. We would like to, for example, correlate paper and pencil tests with interviews, and the reason we would like to do that is that the interviewer gives us this kind of surrogate criterion which we have to use simply because we can't apply any sort of metric to the criterion population and situation. I have another point to make about the problem of the interview technique as a measure. You will recall that Miss Wilds said that the people that give these interviews are instructors in the language, professional linguists and so forth. In this regard Sydney Sako and I had an interesting experience a couple of years ago when we were asked to develop an oral proficiency test in Vietnamese. Since Sydney and I have no knowledge of Vietnamese whatsoever, we had to go to the Vietnamese faculty at DLI and have them construct some sentences and dialogues to certain specifications for us. A Vietnamese Air Force Captain who was working there was approached and said that he'd be perfectly willing to make recordings of these. He went to the studio, and about 20 minutes later he came back, and he said, "I apologize, but I am unable to make these recordings for you." I said "What's the matter, is it bad Vietnamese?" And he said, "Oh no! It's superb Vietnamese, but it is not the way pilots talk. It's the way teachers talk." One of the problems with the interviews is that they are being given by the wrong people. This problem of whether you are going to rate a man down because his grammar is bad or not keeps coming up all the time. I want to find out, can the man cope? I don't care how bad his grammar is, unless there are situations where the social acceptableness of his language does become a factor.

Swift: I just wanted to comment on Professor Oller's question concerning the correlation of grammar and vocabulary. We have observed over the years something that we facetiously call the Peace Corps Syndrome, but it applies to almost any person who comes to be tested, whose formal training has been relatively short, and whose exposure to the language in the field has been comparatively long. I would say there is here a distinct non-correlation between grammar and vocabulary, with the possibility of a wide range of vocabulary used in a very minimal set of grammatical structures. And it is frequently quite good communication. This sometimes raises the problem of whether we are going to apply the same standards in terms of weighting the grammar for this kind of test if what we're really trying to test is communicative ability.

Oller: All I can say is I agree with what Fran Cartier said, and with Spolsky's arguments along those lines. I'm doubtful about the research behind the comment on the lack of correlation between grammar and vocabulary. I think if you have a good vocabulary test and a good grammar test, and if you give it to typical populations of non-native speakers, you'll discover a very high correlation, above the 80% level. And what this suggests to me is that what linguists have encouraged us to believe as two separate functional systems, lexis and grammar, are in fact a whole lot more closely related to some underlying communicative competence. And my argument is that if you do careful research on it, I expect you'll find that those five scales are very closely related. We did a little bit of that at UCLA and discovered that they were indistinguishable for practical purposes on scales of this sort. But that's not published research, and I don't know of any other published research which could be carefully examined and challenged.

Clark: I think quite a lot of the questions here deal with the problem of what is the criterion on which the interview performances are to be rated or evaluated. From my point of view I think the big selling point of the FSI interview is that it permits judgments about the person's ability to do certain things with the language in real-life terms, or at least portions of the interview do. If you look at the scoring system for the FSI, there's some intermingling of competencies in the sense of ordering a meal, finding one's way around, etc., and on the other hand, how much grammar he knows, what his pronunciation is like, and so forth. If it could be possible to weed out the strictly structural aspects of the FSI criteria and stick instead with operational statements of what he can do, then I believe our problem is solved. We use the face-to-face interview of the operational type, and then we correlate the results of this with very highly diagnostic tests of vocabulary, grammar and so forth, and we actually see empirically what the relationships are at different levels of performance.

Spolsky: What we're doing here actually is criticizing the fact that the interview test is not a direct measure but is an indirect measure of something else. I think we can get a clearer view if we add the sociolinguistic dimension that we're talking in. But if we're talking about the situations in which language is going to be used, the conversation that comes up in the interview is only one of those situations. It's clear that one would expect a good correlation between performances in an interview and any other conversations with either language teachers or people who speak like language teachers. But there's the question of doing some of these other functions that could be different. The other point I was going to mention here deals with the problem of correlation between grammar, vocabulary, and performances of various kinds, which is, I think, related to the point that John Oller makes in another paper that I recently read, where he talks about the relevance of the language learning history, and that people who learn a language in different contexts are likely to be better at different parts of language. It is theoretically possible for two people with a vocabulary of 10,000 words to have only—depending on the language—800 of those words in common. It's also going to be theoretically possible that two people will get by in languages making quite distinct basic errors in those languages, and will continue speaking the language for many years still making quite different basic errors. There are certain things that will happen overall that will average out. But when it comes to judging an individual, there's likely to be the effect of two different language learning pasts. I think a comparison of ex-Peace Corps volunteers with normal college foreign language majors would bring this point out extremely clearly. And then there is this whole question of the communication or sociolinguistic analysis of the kinds of predictions you want to make on the basis of the test. When one looks at that second picture, then I think you can argue that the interview test has to be dealt with also as an indirect measure, and one has to decide what is the direct measure against which to correlate it.

Tetrault: How do you combine a functional evaluation with a check of specific points of structure? How do you elicit points of structure?

Wilds: For example, eliciting a subjunctive that hasn't occurred naturally might happen in an interpreting situation, where you have the examinee ask the other examiner, "He wants to know if it's possible for you to come back later." So that if at all possible all structural elements are elicited in the context of some functional problem.

Tetrault: I assume then you'd have to, in some cases, elicit it from English rather than the language.

Wilds: That's right, and that's why I think there's an advantage in having one examiner who speaks English natively. He can set up a situation in a very natural context. We never require formal interpreting; it's never set up to be a word-for-word thing.

Testing Communicative Competence in Listening Comprehension

Peter J. M. Groot

1.0. Introduction. Foreign language needs in present-day society have changed greatly during the past 20-30 years. Nowadays much more importance is attached to the ability to speak and understand a foreign language because many more contacts with members of other linguistic communities take place through what is sometimes called the phonic[1] layer of language, i.e. listening and speaking (telephone, television, radio, stays abroad for business and/or recreational purposes, etc.). Changes in foreign language needs accordingly must be reflected in foreign language teaching and testing. This paper gives a rough description of the development of listening comprehension tests to be administered to final year students in some types of secondary schools in Holland. Its purpose is to serve as an example of how tests of communicative ability should be developed, whether it be in a school situation or during a language training program for students who are going to work abroad. Of course, the specific aims of the various educational situations will differ, but the principles underlying the construction of reliable, valid and economical tests largely remain the same.

In 1969 the Ministry of Education asked the Institute of Applied Linguistics of the University of Utrecht to develop listening comprehension tests to be introduced as part of experimental modern foreign language exams (French, German and English) administered at some types of secondary schools.

1.1. Organization. On the basis of an estimate of the activities to be carried out, a team was formed consisting of one teacher of French, one teacher of German, one teacher of English, some project-assistants and a director of research.

1.2. Research plan. The research plan to be followed would roughly comprise three stages: (a) Formulation of an objective for listening comprehension of French, German and English, with interpretation of the term listening comprehension, and formulation of a listening comprehension objective on the basis of (a) and (b); (b) Operationalization of the listening comprehension objective; (c) Validating the operationalisation.

2.0. Formulation of the Objective. The question whether a test is valid cannot be answered if one does not know the objective the test is supposed to measure.[2] Hence, the first stage will have to be the formulation of the objective that should be tested. The official objectives for the teaching of modern languages in the Netherlands, as laid down in official documents, are extremely vague or nonexistent.

Abroad, some attempts have been made to formulate objectives for modern languages but, if listening comprehension is separately specified at all, either the formulation of the objective is much lacking in explicitness or the objective is not relevant to the situation in Holland. As a result, it is not surprising that there are many interpretations of the term listening comprehension being applied in current teaching practice. The first step to be taken in formulating an objective, then, will be to give an interpretation of the term listening comprehension.

2.1. Interpretation of the term listening comprehension. The two guiding principles in formulating any educational objective will be utility and desirability and feasibility. In interpreting the term listening comprehension, therefore, it is necessary to give an interpretation that is both useful and feasible.

How does one arrive at such an interpretation? Our starting point is the premise that the primary function of language is communication, i.e. the transmission and reception of information. The foreign language teacher's task, then, is to teach his pupils to communicate in the foreign language. Consequently, these objectives will have to be descriptions of (levels of) communicative ability.

If we now turn to current listening comprehension teaching and testing practice, we find that it is very often based on interpretations that result in teaching and testing skills, such as dictation or sound discrimination, that cannot properly be called communicative abilities. These may be useful activities during the learning process, but they can hardly be said to constitute communicative abilities in any useful sense of the word. A useful interpretation of the term listening comprehension will thus have a strong communicative bias; in other words, its general meaning will be picking up the information—the auditory messages encoded from presented language-samples.

2.2. Determining the listening comprehension level. The interpretation given in 2.1 to the term listening comprehension was used to construct a test with open-ended questions consisting of language samples that were selected as to their difficulty level on mainly intuitive grounds from a number of sources. The questions measured whether the most important information had been understood. These tests (one each for French, German and English) were administered to some 150 pupils divided among 4 schools. The scores provided evidence in connection with the degree of difficulty of the language-samples that the pupils of the 25 schools taking part in the project could be expected to handle, in other words, what would be feasible.

2.3. Formulation of the listening comprehension objective. Ideally, the process of formulating objectives for the four language skills, (listening, speaking, reading, writing) will pass through five stages: (1) Interpreting the terms listening, speaking, reading, writing, i.e. defining the nature of the skill; (2) Making a typology of the situations in which the students will have to use the foreign language after their school or training period and determining how they will have to use it (receptively and/or productively, written and/or orally); (3) Determining the "linguistic content" of the situations referred to under (2); (4) Determining what is feasible in the school situation; (5) Formulating objectives on the basis of (1) through (4). Much of the work mentioned under (2) and (3) remains to be done. It is therefore clear that formulating a listening comprehension objective was not an easy task.

Using the arguments and findings described in 2.1 and 2.2, the following objective was formulated: The ability to understand English/French/German speech spontaneously produced, at normal conversational tempo, by educated native speakers, containing only lexical and syntactic elements that are also readily understandable to less educated native speakers (but avoiding elements of an extremely informal nature), and dealing with topics of general interest.

2.3.1. Explanatory remarks and comments. The main reason for explicitly defining the language to be understood as speech was the fact that in language teaching written language receives enough emphasis but spoken language is much neglected. Most people will accept that the ability to understand spontaneously produced speech is a desirable objective for French, German and English, one reason being that it is a necessary condition for taking part in a conversation in the foreign language. Now, the spoken language differs in many respects from the written language, mainly because the time for reflection while producing it is much more limited.[3] For this reason, if we want to make sure spoken language is taught and tested, it should be mentioned explicitly in the objective.

A good language teaching objective should explicitly define the language samples that can be put in the test used to measure whether the pupils have (sufficiently) reached the objective. The above listening comprehension objective falls short of this requirement. The spontaneous speech of educated native speakers within the area as defined by the objective will still vary widely as regards speech-rate; lexical, idiomatic and syntactic characteristics; etc.

This means that the limitations mentioned in the objective are not exact enough. To make them more explicit, many questions will have to be answered first, questions such as the following:

• What is normal conversational tempo? We know that there is a large variety in speech-rate between individual native speakers. In a pilot study for English, for example, a range of 11-23 centiseconds per syllable was found.

• What are topics of general interest? The reason for taking up this specification in the objective was to avoid giving one section of the population an advantage over another. It is clear that this element in the objective does not apply to situations where the terminal language behavior aimed at by the course is much more specifiable.

• What syntactic elements are readily understandable to less educated (i.e. without a secondary school education) native speakers? Very little is known about correlates between syntactic complexity and perceptual difficulty. Psycholinguistic research (cf. Bever 1971) has convincingly proved that there are correlates, but in most cases this evidence was found in laboratory experiments with isolated sentences. Even if the internal validity of these experiments is high, the external validity is doubtful; in other words, it is questionable as to how far these findings can be extrapolated to real-life situations.

• What is the effect of limiting the test to educated native speakers (i.e. native speakers with at least a secondary school education)? Educated native speakers are referred to in the objective as a means of limiting the range of accents of the language samples that can be used in the test.

Although answers to the above questions may never be completely satisfactory, the listening comprehension objective formulated in 2.3 does give the teacher and student a much clearer view of what is expected after the secondary school period than did the formulations referred to in 2.0.

3.0. Operationalising the Objective. The fact that the listening comprehension objective formulated in 2.3 is a compromise between what is desirable and useful, on the one hand, and what is feasible, on the other, has implications for the tests that can be considered good operationalisations of the objective. These tests will have the nature of both achievement tests (the feasibility aspect) and proficiency tests (the desirability aspect). An achievement test measures knowledge, insight and skills which the testees can be expected to demonstrate on the basis of a syllabus that has been covered, while proficiency tests measure knowledge, insight and skills, irrespective of a particular syllabus.

Achievement tests are concerned with a past syllabus, while proficiency tests are concerned with measuring abilities that the testee will have to demonstrate in the future. A test, to be used for final examination purposes, will thus have the character of both an achievement and a proficiency test; in other words, it will test what has been learned and what "should" have been learned.

Apart from the above arguments, there is also another, more pragmatic argument to defend final (language) exams having this hybrid character. They could not be achievement tests only, since, in schools where the tests are given, the syllabi vary depending on what textbooks and other course material (readers, articles, etc.) the individual teacher has chosen.[4] One of the consequences of the hybrid nature of the tests operationalising the listening comprehension objective is the fact that teachers cannot restrict themselves to training their students in a particular syllabus. Also, they will have to give proper training in the (behavioural) skills specified in the objective.

3.1. In order to produce a reliable, valid and economical operationalisation of the listening comprehension objective the following demands[5] had to be met in constructing the tests.

3.1.1. The questions in the test should measure whether testees have listened with understanding to the language samples presented. They should not measure knowledge of a particular lexical or syntactic element from the sample, since understanding the sample need not be equivalent to knowing every element in it. Ideally, the semantic essence of the language sample constitutes the correct answer to the test question.

If we want the test to be valid, it is essential for the questions to measure global comprehension of the samples. How this global comprehension is arrived at is largely unknown, because we have no adequate analysis of listening comprehension at our disposal. We know little of the components of listening comprehension and even less of their relative importance. Of course, one can safely say that knowledge of the vocabulary, syntax and phonology of the target-language are important factors. Most language tests limit themselves to measuring these components, but most of the evidence accumulated in recent testing research corroborates the statement that communicative competence (i.e. the ability to handle language as a means of communication) is more than the sum of its linguistic components. For that reason a test of listening comprehension, as described in the objective, cannot be valid if it only measures the testee's command of the (supposed) linguistic components, since its validity correlates with the extent to which it measures the whole construct: both the linguistic and non-linguistic components of listening comprehension.

3.1.2. Since the language samples to be used in the test have to be bits of spontaneous speech, they must be selected from some form of conversation (dialogue, group-discussion, interview, etc.). To ensure this, the samples were selected from recordings of talks between native speakers.

3.1.3. In some real-life listening situations (radio, television, films) the listener will not be in a position to have the message repeated. In other such situations (e.g. conversation), this possibility does exist, but an excessive reliance on it indicates deficient listening comprehension. For this reason (the validity of the test as a proficiency test), it was decided to present the auditive stimuli once only.

3.1.4. Although memory, both short and long term, plays an important role in the listening comprehension process, it should not be heavily taxed in a test of foreign language listening comprehension, when it is familiarity with the foreign language that should be primarily measured. To safeguard this, the length of the language samples was restricted to 30-45 seconds.

3.1.5. Similarly, to ensure that the foreign language listening comprehension test does not excessively emphasize the reasoning component, the concepts presented in the samples should be relatively easy. This can be checked by presenting them to native speakers some two or three years younger than the target population (cf. also 5.3.5).

3.1.6. Since the tests were to be used on large populations, distributed among many schools and teachers, the test questions were of the multiple-choice type. It was found that items consisting of a stem plus three alternatives, instead of the usual four, were most practical.

3.1.7. The multiple-choice questions should be presented in a written form. If they are presented auditorily, test scores may be negatively influenced by the fact that testees fail to understand the questions.

3.1.8. In order to standardise the acoustic conditions of presentation, it was decided to administer the tests in language laboratories to eliminate, as much as possible, sources of interfering noise, both in and out of the classroom.

3.2. Description of the test. Testees, seated in a language laboratory with individual headphones, listen to taped interviews or discussions, which are split up into passages of about 30-45 seconds. Following each passage there is a twenty-second pause in which testees answer on a separate answer sheet a multiple-choice global comprehension question. The test consists of fifty items, takes approximately one hour and comprises three different interviews or discussions. After each part of sixteen to seventeen items, there is a break of at least ten minutes. The tests are pretested on native speakers and Dutch pupils. After item analysis, the final form is administered to the target population in two "scrambled" versions to avoid cheating. The following are examples taken from the examination listening comprehension tests for 1972.

French

Question: Est-ce que le whisky est un concurrent pour les boissons françaises?

Réponse: Vous savez que le whisky a été une des boissons qui s'est le plus développées dans les pays du continent depuis quelques années, c'est devenu une boisson à la mode. Il est certain que cette nouvelle mode a été un concurrent pour certains produits traditionnels français . . . certains apératifs, certains vins, peut-être même nos spiritueux.

Item: Est-ce que le whisky est un concurrent pour les boissons françaises, selon M.J.?

A Non, parce que boire du whisky est une mode que passera.

B Non, parce que le whisky diffère trop des boissons françaises.

C Qui, parce que le whisky a beaucoup de succés actuellement.

English

Question: Talking about newspapers, what do you object to in the presentation of news?

Answer: What I strongly depreciate is an intermingling of news with editorial comment. Editorial comment's terribly er... easy to do, but news and facts are sacred and should be kept at all time quite, quite distinct. I think it's very wrong and you have this in so many newspapers where the editorial complexion or the political complexion of the newspaper determines its presentation of facts, emphasizing what they consider should be emphasized and not emphasizing unhappy facts which conflict with their particular point of view.

Item: What does Mr. Ellison Davis object to in some newspapers?

A That the way they present their news is too complex.

B That the editor presents his opinions as news items.

C That their presentation of facts is influenced by editorial views.

German

Frage: Frau K., Sie sind nun berufstätig. Was denken Sie über die berufstätige Frau mit kleinen Kinder?

Antwort: Da müsste ihr natürlich der Staat sehr viel helfen. Hat diese Frau Kinder dann muss ihr die Möglichkeit geboten werden, das Kind in einen Kindergarten stecken zu können, der a. gut ist, d.h. eine Kindergärtnerin muss für kleine Gruppen da sein, und der den ganzen Tag offen ist, dass sie nicht mittags schnell nach Hause laufen muss um zu sehen, was nun das Kind macht. Ehm, dann ist es wohl möglich, dass sie auch während der Ehe berufstätig ist. Vorausgesetzt natürlich, dass auch der Mann diese Möglichkeit akzeptiert.

Item: Was denkt Frau K. über eine berufstätige Frau mit kleinen Kindern?

A Der Staat sollte ihr das Arbeiten ermöglichen.

B Die Meinung des Mannes verhindert die berufstätigkeit vieler Frauen.

C Nur morgens sollte sie arbeiten, mittags sollte sie für die Kinder da sein.

4.0. Reliability. Since 1969 many listening comprehension tests of the kind described in 3.2 have been constructed and administered. The liability of the tests, as calculated with the Kuder-Richardson 21 formula, ranged from .70 to .80. Taking into account the complexity of the skill measured, these figures can be considered satisfactory. Indeed, it remains to be seen whether listening comprehension tests of this kind can be constructed that show higher reliability coefficients. If not, one of the implications could be that, in calculating correlation coefficients of these tests with other tests, correction for attenuation cannot be applied.

In general, the listening comprehension tests for French show the highest reliability and standard deviations, the tests for German show the lowest and the English tests take a middle position. The figures for the 1972 Fench listening comprehension test shown below may be considered representative for most of the psychometric indices of the listening comprehension tests administered.

Results, English listening comprehension test, 1972

Number of testees	840
Mean score	80%
Standard deviation	11,82
Reliability (KR-21)	.77

5.0. Validity. The listening comprehension objective formulated in 2.3 considerably limits the amount of valid operationalisations, but it still allows for more than one.

We chose the operationalisation described in 3.2 because it best meets both validity and educational requirements. Various questions in connection with its validity can be raised, however. Should the multiple-choice questions be presented before or after listening to the passage? Does the fact that multiple-choice questions are put in the target language affect the scores? Is the use in the distractors of the multiple-choice question of a word (or words) taken from the passage a valid technique? Should the testees be allowed to make notes? How long should the passages (items) of the test be?

The last two questions have been dealt with during discussions with the teachers taking part in the experiment on the basis of their experiences in administering the tests. It was not considered advisable to allow the testees to make notes while listening because this would decrease the attention given to listening. The length of the passages should not exceed 45 seconds in connection with concentration problems (cf. 3.1).

The first three questions have been dealt with in experiments of the following type: a control group and an experimental group were formed, which were comparable as to listening comprehension on the basis of scores on previous listening comprehension tests (equal mean score, standard deviation, etc.). The two groups took the same test in two forms, the difference being the variable to be investigated. The results of experiments carried out in this stage are given below.[6]

Experiment 1

Variable: multiple-choice questions before listening to the passage.

Control group	(85 testees)	Questions after	71%
Experimental group	(85 testees)	Questions before	72%

These data were discussed with the teachers taking part in the experiment, and it was decided to present the questions before listening to the passages. The general feeling was that this technique made the listening activity required more natural and lifelike, because it enabled the testees to listen selectively.

Experiment 2

Variable: multiple choice questions in mother tongue.

Control group	(120 testees)	
Questions in foreign language		77%
Experimental group	(120 testees)	
Questions in mother tongue		82%

During discussions with the teachers, it was decided to present the questions in the foreign language because the pupils preferred it and the difference in the mean scores of the two groups was relatively small.

Experiment 3: Echoic elements

In this experiment the object was to determine the effect of using so-called "echoic" elements in the alternatives of the multiple choice questions. (Echoic elements are words, taken from the passage, that are used in the alternatives.) A twenty-item test was constructed so that the correct alternatives of the items contained hardly any echoic elements—one distractor contained echoic elements, one did not. This test was administered to a group of eighty pupils who had taken other listening comprehension tests. The item analysis of the scores showed an average discrimination value of .41. From this the conclusion was drawn that the use of echoic elements in the distractors (and sometimes in the correct alternative, of course) is indeed a good technique to separate poor from good listeners.

5.1. After evaluating the outcome of the experiments and discussions referred to in 5.0, proper validation of the tests in their final form could start. The tests that were validated were the examination tests of 1971 and 1972.

Following Cronbach's (1966) division, I shall deal with content validity, concurrent validity and construct validity.

5.2. Content validity. What was said in 3.0 about the nature of these tests (partly achievement, partly proficiency) implies that in establishing their content validity there are two questions that have to be dealt with: (1) To what extent do the tests adequately sample the common core of the instructional syllabus the target population has covered? (2) To what extent do the tests adequately sample the listening proficiency described in behavioural terms in the objective?

5.2.1. As regards the first question the intuitions, based on teaching experience of the members of the test construction team about the common core of the syllabi covered by various schools taking part, proved to be highly reliable. Evidence for the reliability was acquired during discussions with the teachers on the tests administered where, only rarely, lexical or syntactic elements in the tests were objected to as being unfair. In this context one has to bear in mind that answering the global comprehension questions correctly does not depend on knowledge of each and every lexical and/or syntactic element (cf. 3.0).

5.2.2. A much more complicated problem is posed by the second question. In the objective, the level of listening comprehension expected of the pupils is described in functional terms. It is an attempt to specify in what sociolinguistic context pupils are expected to behave adequately (i.e. understand the message). It does not give a detailed linguistic description of these sociolinguistic situations. Some linguistic characteristics are given (in connection with lexical and syntactic aspects), but these are not very precise. One of the consequences is that it will be impossible to claim a high content-validity in linguistic terms of a test operationalising the objective.[7] Claims in connection with content-validity will have to be based on evidence concerning the representivity of the situations in the test for the universe of situations described in the objective. For this reason, the TOLC-tests are rather long (fifty items dealing with a range of topics). We are confident that these tests form a representative selection of the situations defined in the objective.

5.3. Concurrent validity. The concurrent validity of the TOLC-tests was investigated in various experiments.

5.3.1. One of the assumptions in connection with the TOLC-tests is that pupils who score high on these tests will understand French, German and English on radio and television better than pupils who score lower. To find out whether this assumption was warranted, a test was constructed consisting of language samples selected from the above sources. This test was administered on a population of pupils that also took a selection of the 1972 TOLC-test.

Results

Selection '72 test:	30 items	Number of pupils:	120
"Radio-test:"	30 items	(p.m.) correlation:	.67

5.3.2. The 1971 and 72 TOLC-tests were correlated with teacher ratings. Some teachers were asked to rate their pupils' listening comprehension on a four-point scale. These pupils also took a TOLC-test, and the teacher ratings were correlated with the scores on the test. The p.m. correlations ranged from .20 to .70. (This lack of consistency may be explained by the fact that listening comprehension as worked out in the TOLC-tests was a relatively new skill to the teachers and hence hard to evaluate.)

5.3.3. On the request of some of the teachers taking part in the project, an experiment was carried out to determine whether the fact that the test questions were of the multiple-choice type influenced the scores in such a way that it would invalidate the test. For this purpose the 1971 and '72 TOLC-tests were used. These two tests can be taken to be of a comparable degree of difficulty, as witnessed the scores of the populations who had taken them as exam tests.

Results

Selection '71:	40 items
Selection '72 (open questions)	
Max. score 60:	60 items
Number of pupils:	90
(p.m.) correlation:	.68

Also, the selection of the 1971 test was correlated with the selection of the 1972 test, presented without any questions. The pupils had to give a summary of the passages listened to. The correlation for English was .69.

5.3.4. The 1971 TOLC-test was correlated with listening comprehension tests developed by the Swedish Department of Education. These tests were similar to the TOLC-tests as far as the presentation of the stimuli and questions were concerned. The language samples were different (e.g. not spontaneously produced speech).

Results

Selection TOLC-test '71	36 items	Number of pupils:	75
Swedish test:	29 items	(p.m.) correlation:	.64

5.3.5. Also, the scores on the foreign language listening comprehension tests have been compared with scores on equivalent comprehension tests in the mother tongue. While the foreign language test scores averaged 70% for Fench, 74% for English and 76% for German, the Dutch test scores averaged 88%. The fact that mother-tongue listening comprehension on higher levels is not perfect has already been shown by other studies (Spearrit 1962; Nichols 1957; Wilkinson 1968). It is reassuring to know, however, that listening efficiency can be improved through relatively simple training procedures (Erickson 1954).

5.3.6. Construct validity. In order to find out more about the construct that had apparently been measured, the TOLC-test scores were correlated with scores on tests of various hypothesised components of listening comprehension. The prediction was that scores on the test of linguistic components (vocabulary, grammar, phonology) would correlate higher with scores on the global listening comprehension tests than would scores on tests of non- or para-linguistic components, such as memory, intelligence, etc.

The linguistic components were tested in various ways (e.g. vocabulary was tested by means of tests presenting isolated words and tests presenting contextualised words). The non-linguistic components were tested by means of standardised tests (Raven's Advanced Progressive Matrices Set I, Auditory Letter Span Test MS-3, etc.). The results showed that the correlations between the non-linguistic subtests and the global listening comprehension tests were indeed much lower (ranging from .07 to .25) than the correlations between the linguistic subtests and the global listening comprehension tests (ranging from .40 to .69).

6.0. Concluding Remarks. I have intentionally refrained from giving a detailed analysis of the above data or suggesting directions for further research into listening comprehension. My main point has been to demonstrate in what way tests can be a vital part of research into communicative competence. Further research might take the form of comparing the overall listening comprehension test scores with results of cloze tests using reduced redundancy. It might take the form of factor analysis of the hundreds of listening comprehension test items that have been administered to see whether any prominent factors emerge and, if so, whether they can be interpreted as parts of a meaningful linguistic or psychological framework. But whatever form it takes, it will be a disciplined activity, testing hypotheses concerning communicative competence conceived on the solid basis of reliable empirical evidence—a basis that seems to be sadly lacking in much research on language learning, resulting in fashionably exchanging one ill-founded opinion for another.

NOTES

1. The phonic layer as opposed to the graphic layer (reading and writing), which was much more the mode of linguistic communication some decades ago.
2. It is not implied here that this is the only condition to be fulfilled in order to establish the validity of a test!
3. Suffice it to mention syntactic irregularities, different choice of words, speech errors, hesitation pauses, etc.
4. Whether these subjectively chosen materials do cover the most frequest and useful words is open to doubt. To remedy this, an attempt will be made to produce, for the various types of schools, lists of words that have more objectively been proved to be useful for secondary school pupils to master.
5. Some to be induced from the objective, others to be added on pragmatic grounds. The list of demands under 3.1 is by no means exhaustive. It only gives the conditions these particular tests had to fulfill. It does not specify the general requirements any good test has to satisfy.
6. For the sake of brevity, the figures for the English test are given, as the figures for the German and French tests yielded very much the same patterns.
7. Even if the objective did give a detailed linguistic description, it would be difficult to establish content validity for a test operationalising it. This is a general problem applicable to all language tests. The root of this problem lies in the generative character of natural language. The rules governing a language are such that an infinite number of possible applications and combinations can be generated by speakers of that language. Consequently it will be difficult to determine whether the content of a test constitutes a representative selection of the possible applications and combinations.

DISCUSSION

Clark: I notice that the one example item that is given is a three-option item. It would be relatively easy to make a fourth or even a fifth option for the item, which, I think, would increase the reliability of the test. We've tried somewhat the same thing at ETS where two or three native language speakers recorded about two or three minutes on topics like pollution, Watergate, and so forth; then multiple-choice questions were asked on the conversation. The reading difficulty problem was overcome by having the questions in the students' native language. We've found that this type of real-life conversational listening comprehension is much more difficult than the discrete item.

Spolsky: Presumably because listening comprehension is the closest to underlying competence—or has the fewest kinds of other performance factors involved—it is least dependent on learning experience. With a certain amount of limited experience or exposure to a language, and a limited learning history that includes exposure to the language, listening comprehension is going to be the one that is closest to the most basic knowledge of a language. It's the first kind of thing that gets developed. It would be unusual to find somebody who is more proficient in speaking than in understanding. If we take a test of listening ability, one would expect to find it correlates more highly with almost every other test than anything else.

Jones: The problem is, of course, to measure the ability. How do you know if the student understood or not? He's got to respond in some way—which means that you're only secondarily getting at the performance.

Cartier: I think Spolsky is trying to get at the problem of the real world where we listen either for information or directions to do something. We process the information in various ways, and the resultant behavior may be immediate or it may be way off in the future. Ideally, we would like to be able to test each of those two things in their real operational time frames, so that if, for example, you're training aircraft mechanics you can tell them, "If you ever run across a situation where a spark plug is in such and such a condition, then do so and so." Then if, two or three weeks later, they run across such a spark plug, will they in fact do such and such? Here you've got the problem of listening comprehension, memory, and a whole raft of other kinds of things that are involved, but certainly listening comprehension is a very strong part of it. In an article of mine in the *TESOL Quarterly* some time back, I reported on criterion-referenced testing which used some surrogate criteria in reference to taking directions: For example, you make a tape recording which says in English "Go and get a 7/16th wrench." In the testing room you have a tool box in which there are a whole bunch of tools, including a 7/16th wrench, and these have numbers on them. The examinee goes to the tool box, picks out the proper things, takes the numbers off, and writes them on his answer sheet. The person has to exhibit the behavior you actually record.

Nickel: I'm interested in Spolsky's question concerning the correlation between listening and speaking. From my own experience, I don't exclude a certain percentage of learner types who have a greater competence in speaking than in listening, especially if two factors are present. One, if the topic of discussion is not familiar to the examinee, and two, if the accent is changed, for example a change from a British to an American accent.

Spolsky: I'm still trying to get at the point of overall proficiency; I'm convinced that there is such a thing. Even taking the accent or the style question, presumably there'd be very few cases where people will develop productive control of several styles before they develop receptive control of a wider range of styles.

Reduced Redundancy Testing: A Progress Report

Harry L. Gradman and Bernard Spolsky

In an earlier paper (Spolsky et al., 1968), some preliminary studies were reported of one technique for testing overall second language proficiency, the use of a form of dictation test with added noise. The purpose of this paper is to reconsider some of the notions of that paper in the light of later research.

The original hypothesis had two parts: the notion of overall proficiency and the value of the specific technique. The central question raised was how well the dictation test with added noise approximates functional tests with clear face validity. There was no suggestion that it could replace either tests of specific language abilities or various functional tests (such as the FSI interview [Jones, forthcoming] or other interview tests [Spolsky et al., 1972]). Research with the test came to have two parallel concerns: an interest in the theoretical implications of the technique, and a desire to investigate its practical value in given situations.

The theoretical issues have now been quite fully discussed (Spolsky, 1971; Oller, 1973; Gradman, 1973; Briere, 1969). Assuming the relevance of what Oller calls a grammar of expectancy, any reduction of redundancy will tend to increase a non-native's difficulty in functioning in a second language more than a native speaker, exaggerating differences and permitting more precise measurement. The major techniques so far investigated for reducing redundancy have been on written cloze tests (Oller, 1973; Darnell, 1970), oral cloze tests (Craker, 1971), and dictation tests with (Spolsky et al., 1968; Whiteson, 1972; Johansson, 1973; Gradman, 1974) and without (Oller, 1971) additional distortion. In this paper, we will discuss some of the more recent studies of the dictation test with added distortion and will consider their theoretical and practical implications.

The original study (Spolsky et al., 1968) described six experiments carried out in 1966 at Indiana University. In a preliminary experiment, fifty sentences from an aural comprehension test were prepared with added white noise. Six students were asked to write down what they heard. There was evidence of correlation between the score on this test and a comprehension score, and non-native speakers of English were clearly separated from natives, but the test seemed too hard: there were too many "tricks" in the sentences, and the signal-to-noise ratios were somewhat uncontrolled. In the second experiment, lack of control of signal-to-noise ratio and dissatisfaction with the sentences again caused concern. In the third preliminary study, sentence content continued to cause confusion, with certain sentences turning out to be easy or hard under any conditions. In the next experiment, the sentences were rewritten with an attempt made to control sentence structure. Following a then current hypothesis suggesting that sentence difficulty was related to the number of transformations undergone, sentences were written in which each sentence had the same number of words, all words were frequent (occurring at least once in every 3000 words, and there were five sentences for each of ten structural descriptions. Groups of 5 sentences were chosen randomly with one sentence from each structural type, and appropriate noise was added. Attention in this experiment was focused on the possibility of learning: did the test get easier as the subject became more accustomed to the noise? By the end of this experiment, the learning question was not answered, but the problem of sentence construction was becoming clearer. It was obvious that sentence structure, semantic acceptability, word frequency, and phonological factors could all play a part besides the noise. At this stage, the effect of reversing the order of the signal-to-noise ratios was tried, and it was determined that learning effects could be discounted if the harder items came first.

The next experiment was a trial of the instrument with 48 foreign students. Correlations were .66 with an aural comprehension test and .62 with an objective paper-and-pencil test, and .40 with an essay. But it still seemed too hard; the mixing remained a problem, and the phonological tricks added too much uncertain difficulty. It was realized that "the phonological 'trick' is itself a form of masking, leaving ambiguity to be clarified by redundant features. Consequently, the addition of acoustic distortion makes interference two-fold" (Spolsky et al., 1968, p. 94). It remained impossible to specify to what extent redundancy had been reduced.

The final experiment in the 1966 series used a set of new sentences (without "tricks") with white noise added electronically. The test was given to 61 foreign students, and correlations of .66 with both the aural comprehension and the discrete item tests and .51 with the essay test resulted. The experiments were summarized as follows:

> These preliminary studies have encouraged us to believe that a test of a subject's ability to receive messages under varying conditions of distortion of the conducting medium is a good measure of his overall proficiency in a language, and that such a test can be easily constructed and administered. (Spolsky et al., 1968, p. 7)

The techniques described in this first paper were tested further in a study reported by Whiteson (1972). Looking for a simple screening device for large numbers of foreign students, Whiteson prepared fifty different sentences on the same structural model as those described above, adding noise to them. The resulting test, which correlated at .54 with another proficiency measure, provided, she felt, evidence of being a good screening device, serving the purposes for which it was intended.

In a somewhat ambitious study of the technique carried out over two years, Johansson investigated not only the overall effect of the test but studied in detail the characteristics of some students with whom it did not work as well. He developed a new form of the test with a number of basic changes: (1) the signal-to-noise ratios were lower, because his Swedish students were, he believed, better than the average foreign students in the Indiana studies; (2) there were fewer sentences; (3) the sentences were written with high redundancy (presumably balancing the effect of the lower signal-to-noise ratios); (4) elements were included that could be expected to cause difficulty for Swedes (supposedly on the basis of some sort of contrastive analysis); (5) the scoring system was changed; and (6) the difficulty order was reversed. With all these changes, and with the probability that the subjects were more homogeneous in English knowledge than those in the Indiana study, the test still showed a reasonably good correlation (.52) with a test that appears (as far as one can tell from the description) to have been a traditional test of knowledge of standard written English. Unfortunately, however, this latter test appears to have been unreliable. The dictation test also correlated well with a phoneme discrimination test. The rest of Johansson's study was concerned with those students for whom the dictation test fails to be a good predictor of academic success. Here he finds some evidence suggesting that there are certain kinds of students whose personality reacts to tests of this kind (whether because of noise alone or the general novelty) and for whom the results are therefore questionable.

Johansson's study raises a number of interesting questions. Obviously, it would be desirable to know the effect of the various changes he made in the form of the test. And his somewhat extreme conclusions appear to be premature; a dictation test without noise but under any conditions of pressure is just as much a test of reduced redundancy as one with noise, so that the theoretical difference may be nil.

In a somewhat more useful assessment of reduced redundancy tests, John Clark (forthcoming) suggests that they can be considered as one kind of indirect proficiency test. This classification is based on the fact that they do not need to reflect normal language use situations, but can be justified by other kinds of validity besides face validity. He feels that there has been sufficient evidence of concurrent validity to warrant "some optimism" that indirect measures might be efficient and economical ways of estimating real-life proficiency, but he points out three major cautions. First, the indirect measures have only been compared with other measures which do not themselves have high face validity. Secondly, the result of an indirect measure might need to be corrected for the subject's language learning history: a written cloze test will not necessarily predict well the performance of a student who has had a purely oral approach. And thirdly, indirect measures will need full explanation to the users of the relation of their results to more obvious tests.

Some additional sets of data have been examined over the past year, suggestive of the continued belief in the dictation test with added noise or the noise test, as it is often called, as an effective instrument in the evaluation of overall language proficiency. Data gathered during January and February of 1974 from three quite different groups of subjects compare favorably with similar data previously reported on (Gradman, 1974).

Perhaps the most thorough analysis of the noise test has been made of 26 Saudi Arabian students enrolled in a special English Skills Program at Indiana University. The students, all of whom began their coursework in January of 1974, were given the noise test, the TOEFL test, the Ilyin Oral Interview, and the Grabal Oral Interview. A multiple-choice version of the noise test was used in which students were asked to select from five choices the closest approximation of a sentence heard on tape with background distorting noise. Fifty such sentences were included and, in fact, were the final sentences of the 1966 experiments. Most correlations were strong enough to suggest a positive relationship between performance on the noise test and the other instruments. The noise test, for instance, correlated at .75 with the total TOEFL score, the highest correlation of the noise test with any other test or TOEFL subtest. In fact, with the exception of the TOEFL English Structure and Writing subtests (.44 and .33 respectively), all correlations were above .60. Interestingly enough, vocabulary and noise correlated at .73, which was not particularly expected, nor was the .68 correlation of the reading comprehension subtest of TOEFL and the noise test. The correlation of .69 between the noise test and the Ilyin Oral Interview—a test consisting of pictures and specific questions, the answers to which are recorded by the interviewer—was the highest of any of the Ilyin correlations. The correlation of the Ilyin Oral Interview with the Grabal Oral Interview—a test of free conversation rated on a 9 point scale for 10 categories by two independent judges—for instance, was only at the .59 level and with the TOEFL total score at the .54 level. On the other hand, the Grabal Oral Interview correlated somewhat similarly to the noise test. For instance, the Grabal and TOEFL total correlated at .73, vocabulary at .71. The writing section of the TOEFL correlated at a particularly low level .17 with the Grabal, but this was not unexpected. Nor was the .38 correlation with the Reading Comprehension subtest of TOEFL. In a comparison of intercorrelations between parts of the TOEFL test, the Ilyin, Grabal, and noise tests, the only higher correlations were between the TOEFL total and listening comprehension subtests (.89) and the TOEFL total and vocabulary subtest (.85). At the very least, the noise test appeared to correlate better with discrete item tests (such as the TOEFL) than did either the Ilyin Oral Interview or the Grabal Oral Interview, both of which may be said to be more functionally oriented than the TOEFL test. By examining the set of intercorrelation data, the noise test appears to function fairly impressively and, in fact, to potentially bridge a gap left otherwise unattended to by the relatively less structured Ilyin and Grabal tests. This, on the other hand, should not be particularly surprising as the nature of the multiple-choice form of the noise test seems to be a cross between functional and discrete-point orientation, thus potentially explaining its stronger correlations with the TOEFL test.

The figures do not differ much from those reported earlier (Gradman, 1974) when 25 Saudi Arabian students were administered the noise test, the Grabal Oral Interview, and the TOEFL test. TOEFL and noise test correlations, for example, were .66 for overall performance and .75 for listening comprehension. The Grabal Oral Interview and noise test correlations were at the .79 level.

The noise test was given to a class of Indiana University graduate students in language testing in February of 1974. They were first given the multiple-choice answer booklet (Form B) and asked to simply mark the correct answers. The purpose of this blind-scoring technique was to determine whether or not the answers were so obvious that the test booklet, at least, needed considerable revision. At first examination, the results were somewhat disheartening. Of the 33 students who took the test under these conditions, the mean level of performance was 29 out of a possible 50, with a range of 30 (high of 38, low of 8), and even reliability (Kuder Richardson, p. 21) was .56, somewhat higher than we sometimes get on "real tests."

However, when the test was given again with the actual test sentences with added distortion, the results were quite different. The correlation between Form B with noise and Form B via Blind Scoring was only .25, a figure which seems reasonable. It suggests, in fact, that there is some relationship, though limited, between the ability to pick out grammatical responses from a list of choices and performance on a test with reduced redundancy. We would have been surprised had the results been far different. Similar results were also obtained when we correlated performance on the Blind Scoring of Form B with Form A of the noise test, in which students are asked to write what they heard over the tape—a straight dictation version with additional noise in the background. Once again the correlation was .25.

Form A of the noise test was given as a dictation exercise to 34 of the same group of students. Using the scoring method described in Spolsky et al (1968), the top 17 scores were made by native speakers of English, and the bottom 17 scores were made by non-native speakers of English. These results were, of course, exactly as we had hoped. The dictation version of the noise test discriminated between native and non-native speakers of English.

Form B of the noise test, the multiple-choice answer version, was given to the same group of students; and once again, the top 17 scores were made by native speakers of English and the bottom 17 scores were made by non-native speakers of English. As with the dictation version, the multiple-choice version of the noise test discriminated between native and non-native speakers.

An interesting additional question, of course, was the relationship between performance on Form A and on Form B of the noise test. At first, when all scores were examined, they correlated at .80, a reasonably high figure. However, when we compared the performance of the non-native speakers alone, ignoring the minor readjustment of native speaker rankings, the correlation was found to be .89, a reasonably good indication that both Forms A and B of the noise test were measuring the same thing.

When we compare the results of performance on the noise test with the results of that of a similar mixed group in 1973, we find them to be almost the same. Correlations between Form A and B were at the .86 level, and both forms of the noise test discriminated appropriately between native and non-native speakers of English (Gradman, 1974).

The results of an examination of the performance of 71 non-native speakers of English who were given Form A of the noise test in January of 1974 and the Indiana University placement examination remain positive. The noise test correlated reasonably well with the Indiana placement examination. The test correlated at .63 with the English structure subtest, with correlations progressively lower for the vocabulary subtest, .52, phonology, .47, and reading comprehension, .37. The correlation with the overall test total was .56. While there is, of course, an indication of relationship between the two instruments, there are a variety of reasons to expect these figures to be a bit lower than some of the others that we have seen, not the least of which is the somewhat different nature of the Indiana placement examination itself. The phonology section of the test, for instance, is a paper and pencil discrete item test which may or may not have anything to do with one's performative aural-oral skills. The reading comprehension section of the test is particularly difficult, extending, we believe, beyond the question of whether or not a student has the ability to read. Perhaps the two best sections of the test—the structure and vocabulary sections, which are somewhat contextually oriented—did indicate stronger correlations.

A not unexpected result was the strong relationship between performance on the first forty sentences of Form A, the dictation version, and the last 10 sentences. It will be remembered from earlier discussions (Spolsky et al., 1968; Gradman, 1974) that the first 40 seconds are characterized by varying degrees of low signal-to-noise ratios, while the last 10 sentences are characterized by a high signal-to-noise ratio, i.e. the last 10 sentences do not appear to be accompanied by any distorting noise. In fact, the correlation between sentences 1-40 and 41-50 was .93, which may lead one to believe that as an overall measure of language proficiency, the noise test might just as well be given as a dictation test without the added distorting noise. Such a correlation is, however, a bit deceptive in terms of the analysis of performance on the sentences themselves. The average percentage correct for sentences 1-40 differs considerably from that of sentences 41-50, 39% as opposed to 57%, a difference of 18%. (In a similar comparison, Whiteson noted a difference of 12% in her version of the test, which had a somewhat different marking system.) In other words, the question may not be one of replacement but rather of the meaning of errors on individual sentences with particular signal-to-noise relationships. That is, we remain interested in trying to determine just exactly what difficulties the language user incurs at particular levels of reduced redundancy. How much redundancy is necessary for different kinds of language ability, and what linguistic units relate to levels of reduced redundancy? The theoretical and applied potential remains for the testing technique, regardless of the fact that similar overall results might well be obtainable from dictation tests alone.

Though we have still barely scratched the surface in terms of work to be done on the noise test, the results thus far have been highly encouraging. There are some very basic things right with it: the noise test separates native and non-native speakers without fail, it correlates reasonably well with other measures of language proficiency, and it appears to be particularly good in its discrimination of weak and strong non-native speakers of English. This is in a test which can be given and marked in a minimum of time with a minimum of difficulty.

REFERENCES

Brière, Eugene J. "Current Trends in Second Language Testing," *TESOL Quarterly* 3:4

(December 1969), 333-40.

Clark, John. "Psychometric Perspectives in Language Testing." To appear in Spolsky, Bernard (ed.), *Current Trends in Language Testing.* The Hague: Mouton, forthcoming.

Craker, Hazel V. "Clozentropy Procedure or an Instrument for Measuring Oral English Competencies of First Grade Children." Unpublished Ed.D. dissertation, University of New Mexico, 1971.

Darnell, Donald K. "Clozentropy: A Procedure for Testing English Language Proficiency of Foreign Students," *Speech Monographs* 37:1 (March 1970), 36-46.

Gradman, Harry L. "Fundamental Considerations in the Evaluation of Foreign Language Proficiency." (Paper presented at the International Seminar on Language Testing, jointly sponsored by TESOL and the AILA Commission on Language Tests and Testing, May 11, 1973, San Juan, Puerto Rico.)

———. "Reduced Redundancy Testing: A Reconsideration." In O'Brien, M.E. Concannon (ed.), *Second Language Testing: New Dimensions.* Dublin: Dublin University Press, 1974.

Ilyin, Donna. *Ilyin Oral Interview.* (Experimental edition.) Rowley, Mass.: Newbury House, 1972.

Johansson, Stig. "An Evaluation of the Noise Test: A Method for Testing Overall Second Language Proficiency by Perception Under Masking Noise," *IRAL* 11:2 (May 1973), 107-133.

Jones, Randall. "The FSI Interview." To appear in Spolsky, Bernard (ed.), *Current Trends in Language Testing.* The Hague: Mouton, forthcoming.

Oller, John W., Jr. "Dictation as a Device for Testing Foreign Language Proficiency," *English Language Teaching* 25:3 (June 1971), 254-259.

———. "Cloze Tests of Second Language Proficiency and What They Measure," *Language Learning* 23:1 (June 1973), 105-118.

Spolsky, Bernard. "Reduced Redundancy as a Language Testing Tool." In Perren, G.E. and Trim, J.L.M. (eds.), *Applications of Linguistics: Selected Papers of the Second International Congress of Applied Linguistics, Cambridge 1969.* London: Cambridge University Press, 1971, 383-390.

———, Bengt Sigurd, Masahito Sako, Edward Walker and Catherine Arterburn. "Preliminary Studies in the Development of Techniques for Testing Overall Second Language Proficiency," *Language Learning* 18, Special Issue No. 3, (August 1968), 79-101.

———, Penny Murphy, Wayne Holm and Allen Ferrel. "Three Functional Tests of Oral Proficiency," *TESOL Quarterly* 6:3 (September 1972), 221-236.

Whiteson, Valerie. "The Correlation of Auditory Comprehension with General Language Proficiency," *Audio-Visual Language Journal* 10:2 (Summer 1972), 89-91.

DISCUSSION

Tetrault: Could you comment on correlations with direct measures?

Gradman: You may recall what I mentioned about the Grabal oral interview, which was in fact simply an oral interview test. The noise test correlated at .64 with that particular measurement, which we thought was a fairly strong correlation. That is as direct a measure as we have. The Ilyin oral interview, which some people are a little negative about, with pictures and particular sentences that you have to ask questions about, showed a little higher correlation, .69. But this test, as I mentioned, seemed to bridge a gap between direct and other indirect measures.

Clark: I believe you said you had the highest correlations between the noise test and the TOEFL. This might be explained by the fact that the TOEFL itself has high internal reliability, and it may well be that if you were to correct the criterion for unreliability in the Ilyin oral interview and other direct tests, you would get even more favorable correlations than are indicated here.

Lado: How was the test scored?

Gradman: We scored five points in the dictation version if everything was correct. We ignored spelling and punctuation. Four points for one error. Anything more than one error, all the way down to simply one word right, was one point. Nothing right was zero. In other words, we used 5, 4, 1, and 0. But the correlations between this and the multiple-choice version, where we simply gave one point if it was picked correctly from five alternatives, were quite high. We haven't compared it with Johannson's system, which is a bit different. I think his was 3, 2, 1.

Lado: We all seem to have accepted the idea that looking at a picture and talking about it is an indirect technique. I don't think it's indirect at all.

Spolsky: I'd like to take up that question of what an indirect or direct technique is. It's possible to think up real-life contexts in which something like the noise test occurs; in other words, listening to an announcement in an airport, or trying to hear an item on the news when the radio is fuzzy. So one can, in fact, say that even this indirect measure can be considered a direct measure of a very specific functional activity. The question then becomes, how widely a single kind of measure like this will correlate with all the others. What interested us initially was the notion of overall proficiency, which we thought was something that should correlate with general language knowledge. We added the noise in hopes of getting some agreement with information theory's models of being able to actually add redundancy in a technically measurable way. In this way you can say that the testee's knowledge of the language is equivalent to adding so much redundancy, or even carrying it through to questions of intelligibility, and that this accent is an intelligible equivalent to the following kind of noise.

Jones: What's your definition of overall proficiency?

Spolsky: It's something that presumably has what Alan Davies would call construct validity. In other words, it depends on a theoretical notion of knowledge of a language and the assumption that while this knowledge at a certain level can be divided up into various kinds of skills, there is something underlying the various skills which is obviously not the same as competence. You have to allow, of course, for gross differences. For example, if somebody is deaf he won't be very good at listening, if somebody hasn't learned to read or write he won't be good at reading or writing, and if somebody has never been exposed to speech of a certain variety he won't be good at handling that. And after allowing for those gross, very specific differences of experience, whatever is left is overall proficiency.

Anon: What is reduced redundancy?

Gradman: Presumably language is redundant, that is, there are a variety of clues in a sentence. By adding noise to the background, it's possible that some of the structural features, at least, may be obscured, but the message may still come through. As a matter of fact, the test shows the point at which native speakers can operate with less of the message than non-native speakers need. Presumably that means that language is redundant enough so that, when only part of the message comes through, it can still be interpreted by a native speaker but not by a non-native speaker. It's kind of the experience you get sometimes when you listen to the radio and there's static in the background, but you can still hear the message. A lot of people complain about having to talk to non-native speakers over the telephone, because the phone itself is just an acoustical device and they can't understand them nearly as well as they can face-to-face.

Cartier: In the 1940s there was a considerable amount of research done by Bell Telephone Laboratories and other people on the redundancy in the sound signal, in the acoustic signal of speech. One of the things they did, for example, was to take tape recordings and go through and clip out little chunks. The indications were then that the acoustic signal contains twice as much acoustic information as is necessary for a native speaker of the language to understand a telephone message. There are other ways that language is redundant besides acoustically. We use an s ending for verbs when the subject is *he*, for example, though the *he* itself indicates that that's third person, making the s on the end of the verb redundant. One way to reduce the redundancy, then, would be to knock off that morpheme. There are many ways you can reduce the redundancy in the language, and still have it intelligible to native speakers. And what Spolsky is trying to do is experiment with various kinds of reduction of that redundancy to see what it does in the testing situation.

Davies: I'd like to ask whether the experiments with reduced redundancy have concentrated on the facts of the message, or whether you're also taking into account the attitudes of communication, whether it's the total communication or just the bones of the message?

Spolsky: Most of the work with the noise test has been done with single sentences, and with simply the ability to recognize those sentences or to write them down. Until one moves into larger contexts, which I understand is planned, it would be impossible to get into any of these other aspects.

Risen: Earlier someone suggested just introducing noise on every tenth word, and I wondered if that might not be introducing more variables than it controls. I'm thinking about some studies that were done with introducing clicks, where it was found that, if the clicks occurred near a syntactic boundary, it introduced less interference than otherwise.

Spolsky: Presumably, if you do this in a statistical way—randomly—with these noises appearing in a statistical rather than in a linguistic pattern, you'll overcome the effect of that phenomenon if it does work the same way as in a cloze test. You can do it where you take out certain parts of speech, but that's a very different kind of cloze test from one where you take out every fifth or sixth word, and certain of these words that get taken out happen to be harder than other words for very good reasons. As long as you're adding the thing randomly in a statistical way, you're breaking across any of these linguistic principles or averaging them out.

Garcia-Zamor: I'd like to address my question to the person who said earlier, "I believe in overall proficiency." I wanted to ask you precisely in which way you see that overall proficiency might differ from the sum or average of one's competence in the different aspects of language that you might be able to isolate? Unless it's significantly different from that, I don't see any meaning in the term "overall proficiency."

Spolsky: It should be obvious by now that I can't say that precisely, or I would have. It's an idea that I'm still playing with. It has to correlate with the sum of various kinds of things in some way, because it should underlie any specific abilities. In other words, I have the notion that ability to operate in a language includes a good, solid central portion (which I'll call overall proficiency) plus a number of specific areas based on experience and which will turn out to be either the skill or certain sociolinguistic situations. Given a picture like that, one can understand why there are such good correlations between almost any kind of language test and any other kind of language test. Why, in fact, one is surprised at not finding correlations. I'm told that of all the tests that ETS has, the ones in which they get the highest internal reliabilities are language tests. Theoretically, at least, two people could know very different parts of a language and, having a fairly small part in common, still know how to get by. That's where overall proficiency becomes important.

Clark: I basically agree with that. But then we come back to the question of what the specific learning history of the student is, and I could see a situation in which the teacher wouldn't say a word in the foreign language during the entire course but would show printed materials with English equivalents, for example. Then if a listening comprehension test were to be given at the end of that particular course, I don't think we would have the general proficiency you're talking about.

Spolsky: The question is, "How do you capture overall proficiency?" Taking the two kinds of measures that theoretically are closest to it—the dictation with or without noise and the cloze test (which for good theoretical reasons are both cases of reduction of redundancy)—it's quite obvious that a student who has never learned to read won't do anything very intelligible with the cloze test. And the same is obvious with a student who has never heard the language spoken: he won't do anything intelligent with the noise test. But excluding these extreme cases, you would assume that there is a fairly large group with minimal knowledge of each that will show up well in the middle.

Stevick: I wonder if there is anything relevant from the Peace Corps experience, where we had fairly large numbers of people coming in who had studied French or Spanish; who on initial testing turned out to be 0 or 0+, apparently not much better than an absolute beginner; but who, when exposed to the spoken language, bloomed rather rapidly? That may be another example of the same thing.

Spolsky: That would be equivalent to a situation in which someone is exposed to the traditional method of learning a language, that is, a grammar-translation approach at school, and then goes to live in the country for two months. At the beginning of the two months that person would test out completely at 0 or something on any kind of oral test. But he already has this overall proficiency that is just waiting for new experiences.

Rolff: Mr. Gradman, you mentioned five types of sentences, but could you mention specifically what types of sentences, and why you chose to use them in the reduced redundancy test?

Gradman: Those were actually Spolsky's sentences back in 1966. The initial study, by the way, is reported in Special Issue Number 3 of *Language Learning*, 1968. There were simple negatives, simple negative questions, simple questions, simple passives, a category called embedded, embedded negatives, embedded questions, embedded questions signaled by intonation only, embedded negative questions, and a category called miscellaneous.

Spolsky: Those with memories that go back to 1965-66 will remember that in those days we were talking of models of grammar that assumed that sentence difficulty could be described by the number and kind of transformations.

Rashbaum: I was very curious about the type of noise that was used to distort the speech, and I was wondering whether actual distortion by varying the pitch or other things had been considered in reduced redundancy?

Spolsky: We tried a number of different kinds of noise at one stage. We found that, for the person taking the test, the most difficult of these was, in fact, background conversation, especially when it was in the subject's native language. But then we decided to use white noise, which seemed to have all the sort of basic characteristics to do the job. Somebody else suggested pink noise. I'm not sure of the difference; I'm told that it might have been better for this sort of thing.

Anon.: What is white noise?

Cartier: White noise sounds like this: sh/sh/sh/sh/sh. It's simply random frequencies at random amplitudes, the basic kind of noise that you hear in back of radio broadcasts. It's called white because it has the same characteristics as white light, that is, all frequencies are represented at random. I guess pink noise is just a little more regular in frequency.

Rickerson: I think it's demonstrable that reduced redundancy testing will, in fact, distinguish native speakers from non-native speakers. Could you comment further on the applicability of that type of testing, though, to establishing the gradations of 1, 2, 3, 4, 5 in proficiency? It would seem rather difficult to do.

Gradman: We found it performs fairly well in terms of separating out the very good and the very bad. We have trouble in the middle.

Dictation: A Test of Grammar Based Expectancies

John W. Oller, Jr. and Virginia Streiff*

I. DICTATION REVISITED

Since the publication of "Dictation as a Device for Testing Foreign Language Proficiency" in *English Language Teaching* (henceforth referred to as the 1971 paper),[1] the utility of dictation for testing has been demonstrated repeatedly. It is an excellent measure of overall language proficiency (Johansson 1974; Oller 1972a, 1972b) and has proved useful as an elicitation technique for diagnostic data (Angelis 1974). Although some of the discussion concerning the validity of dictation has been skeptical (Rand 1972; Breitenstein 1972), careful research increasingly supports confidence in the technique.

The purpose of this paper is to present a re-evaluation of the 1971 paper. That data showed the Dictation scores on the *UCLA English as a Second Language Placement Examination (UCLA ESLPE 1)* correlated more highly with Total test scores and with other Part scores than did any other Part of the ESLPE. The re-evaluation was prompted by useful critiques (Rand 1972; Breitenstein 1972). An error in the computation of correlations between Part (subtest) scores and Total scores in that analysis is corrected; additional information concerning test rationale, administration, scoring, and interpretation is provided; and finally, a more comprehensive theoretical explanation is offered to account for the utility of dictation as a measure of language proficiency.

In a *Reader's Letter*, Breitenstein (1972) commented that many factors which enter into the process of giving and taking dictation were not mentioned in the 1971 paper. For example, there is "the eyesight of the reader" (or the "dictator" as Breitenstein terms him), the condition of his eye glasses (which "may be dirty or due for renewal"), "the speaker's diction," (possibly affected by "speech de-

*We wish to thank Professor Lois McIntosh (UCLA) for providing us with a detailed description of the test given in the fall of 1968. It is actually Professor McIntosh whose teaching skill and experience supported confidence in dictation that is at base responsible for not only this paper but a number of others on the topic. We gratefully acknowledge our indebtedness to her. Without her insight into the testing of langauge skills, the facts discussed here, which were originally uncovered more or less by accident in a routine analysis, might have gone unnoticed for another 20 years of discrete-point testing.

fects or an ill-fitting denture"), "the size of the room," "the acoustics of the room," or the hearing acuity of the examinees, etc. The hyperbole of Breitenstein's facetious commentary reaches its asymptote when he observes that "Oller's statement that 'dictation tests a broad range of integrative skills' is now taking on a wider meaning than he probably meant."

Quite apart from the humor in Breitenstein's remarks, there is an implied serious criticism that merits attention. The earlier paper did not mention some important facts about how the dictation was selected, administered, scored, and interpreted. We discuss these questions below.[2]

Rand's critique (1972) suggests a re-evaluation of the statistical data reported in the 1971 paper. Rand correctly observes that the intercorrelations between Part scores and the Total score on the *UCLA ESLPE 1* were influenced by the weighting of the Part scores. (See the discussion of the test Parts and their weighting below.) In order to achieve a more accurate picture of the intercorrelations, it is necessary to adjust the weightings of the Part scores so that an equal number of points are allowed on each subsection of the test, or alternatively to systematically eliminate the Part scores from the Total score for purposes of correlation.

II. RE-EVALUATION OF DATA DISCUSSED IN THE 1971 PAPER

We will present the re-evaluation of the data from the 1971 paper in three parts: (1) a more complete description of the tested population and the rationale behind the test (in response to Breitenstein 1972), (2) a more complete description of the test, and (3) a new look at the Part and Total score correlations (in response to Rand 1972).

Population and Test Rationale

The *UCLA ESLPE 1* was administered to about 350 students in the fall of 1968. A sample of 102 students was selected. They were representative of about 50 different language backgrounds. About 70 percent of them were males, and 30 percent females. Approximately 60 percent of the students were graduates, while the remainder were undergraduates with regular or part-time status. (See Oller 1972c for a description of a similar population tested in the fall of 1970.)

The objective of the test is to measure English language proficiency for placement purposes. Students who have near native speaker proficiency are exempted from ESL courses and are allowed to enroll in a full course load in their regular studies. Those students who have difficulties with English are required to take one or more courses in remedial English and may be limited to a smaller course load in their regular course of study.

Prior to 1969 when the research reported in the 1971 paper was carried out, the *UCLA ESLPE 1* had never been subjected to the close empirical scrutiny of any statistical analysis. It had been assumed earlier that Part I measured skills closely associated with reading comprehension, Part II indicated how well students could handle English structure, Part III was a good measure of essay writing ability, Part IV tested discrimination skills in the area of sounds, and Part V was a good measure of spelling and listening comprehension. The extent of overlap between the various Parts, and the meaning of the Total score, were actually unknown. The intent of the test was to provide a reliable and valid estimate of overall skill in English along with diagnostic information concerning possible areas of specific weakness.

It would not be difficult to formulate criticisms of the test as a whole and its particular subsections independent of any statistical analysis. This is not the concern of this paper, however. What we are interested in are answers to the following questions. Given the several parts of the *UCLA ESLPE 1*, what was the amount of overlap between them? Was there one subtest that provided more information than the rest? Should any one or more subtests have been replaced or done away with? These are some of the concerns that prompted the analysis presented in the 1971 paper and which, together with the observations stated earlier in this paper, motivated the computations reported here.

Description of the Test: UCLA ESLPE 1

The *UCLA ESLPE 1* consists of five parts. Part I, a Vocabulary Test of 20 items, requires the student to match a word in a story-like context with a synonym. For example:

But the frontier *fostered* positive traits too....	____FOSTERED (A) discouraged (B) promoted (C) adopted

The student reads the context and then selects from (A), (B), or (C) the one that most nearly matches the meaning of the stem word FOSTERED.

Part II is a Grammar Test of 50 items. Each item asks the student to select the most acceptable sentence from three choices. For instance:

(A) The boy's parents let him to play in the water.
(B) The boy's parents let him play in the water.
(C) The boy's parents let him playing in the water.

Part III is a Composition. Students were instructed:

> Write a composition of 200 words, discussing ONE of the following topics. Your ideas should be clear and well organized. When you have finished, examine your paper carefully to be sure that your grammar, spelling and punctuation are correct. Then count the number of words. PLACE A LARGE X after the two hundredth word (200). If you have written fewer than 200 words give the exact number at the end of your composition. Choose ONE and ONLY ONE of the following topics:
>
> 1. An interesting place to visit in my country.
> 2. Advances in human relations in our time.
> 3. A problem not yet solved by science.
> 4. The most popular sport in my country.

Part IV, Phonology, tests perception of English sounds. It consists of 30 tape recorded items. The student hears a sentence on tape. The sentence contains one of two words that are similar phonologically, e.g. *long* and *wrong* as in "His answer was (A) *long* (B) *wrong*." The student has a written form of the sentence on the test paper and must decide which of the two words were on the tape.

Part V is a Dictation. The Dictation is actually in two sections. The two passages selected are each about 100 words in length. One is on a topic of general interest; the other has a science-oriented focus. The material selected for the Dictation is language of a type college-level students are expected to encounter in their course of study. The student is given the following instructions in writing and on tape:

> The purpose of this dictation exercise is to test your aural comprehension and spelling of English. First, listen as the instructor reads the selection at a normal rate. Then proceed to write as the instructor begins to read the selection a second time sentence by sentence. Correct your work when he reads each sentence a third time. The instructor will tell you when to punctuate.

The student then hears the dictation on tape. The text for the *UCLA ESLPE 1* follows:

(1)

> There are many lessons which a new student has to learn when he first comes to a large university. Among other things he must adjust himself to the new environment; he must learn to be independent and wise in managing his affairs; he must learn to get along with many people. Above all, he should recognize with humility that there is much to be learned and that his main job is to grow in intellect and in spirit. But he mustn't lose sight of the fact that education, like life, is most worthwhile when it is enjoyed.

(2)

In scientific inquiry, it becomes a matter of duty to expose a supposed law to every kind of verification, and to take care, moreover, that it is done intentionally. For instance, if you drop something, it will immediately fall to the ground. That is a very common verification of one of the best established laws of nature—the law of gravitation. We believe it in such an extensive, thorough, and unhesitating manner because the universal experience of mankind verifies it. And that is the strongest foundation on which any natural law can rest.

The scoring of Parts I-III, all of which were multiple-choice questions, was purely objective. Each item in Part I was worth 1 point, the whole section being worth 20 points. Items in Part II were each worth ½ point, making the whole section worth 25 points. Part III was worth 15 points, with each item valued at ½ point each.

Parts IVand V require more explanation. Part IV was worth a total of 25 points with each error subtracting ½ point. Students who made more than 50 errors (with a maximum of 1 error per word attempted) were given a score of 0. There were no negative scores, i.e. if a student made 50 errors or more, he scored 0. Spelling errors were counted along with errors in word order, grammatical form, choice of words, and the like. If the student wrote less than 200 words, his errors were pro-rated on the basis of the following formula: Number of words written by the student ÷ 200 words = Number of errors made by the student ÷ X.

The variable X is the pro-rated number of errors, so the student's pro-rated score would be 25 - (½)X. For example, if he wrote 100 words and made 10 errors, by the formula X = 20, his score would be 25 - ½(20) = 15 points. The scoring of Part IV involved a considerable amount of subjective judgment and was probably less reliable than the scoring of any of the other sections.

A maximum of 15 points was allowed for the Dictation. Clear errors in spelling (e.g. *shagrin* for *chagrin*), phonology (e.g. *long hair* for *lawn care*), grammar (e.g. *it became* for *it becomes*), or choice of wording (e.g. *humanity* for *mankind*) counted as ¼ point subtracted from the maximum possible score of 15 points. A maximum of ¼ point could be subtracted for multiple errors in a single word, e.g. an extra word inserted into the text which was ungrammatical, misspelled, and out of order would count as only one error. If the student made 60 errors or more on the Dictation, a score of 0 was recorded. Alternative methods of scoring are suggested by Valette (1967).

Part and Total Intercorrelations on the UCLA ESLPE 1

The surprising finding in the 1971 paper was that the Dictation correlated better with each other Part of the *UCLA ESLPE 1* than did any other Part. Also, Dictation correlated at .86 with the Total score, which was only slightly less than the correlation of .88 between the Total and the Composition score. What these data suggested was that the Dictation was providing more information concerning the totality of skills being measured than any other Part of the test. In fact, it seemed to be tapping an underlying competence in English.

The data presented in the 1971 paper, however, have been questioned by Rand (1972). As mentioned earlier, Rand (1972) correctly observes that the weightings of Part scores will affect their correlation with the Total score. Obviously, there is perfect correlation between the portion of the Total score and the Part score to which it corresponds. Also, differential weightings of scores will have slight effects on Part and Total correlations even if the self-correlations are systematically eliminated. If Part scores are unevenly weighted (which they were in the 1971 paper), the intercorrelations between Part scores and the Total will be misleading.

One way of removing the error is to adjust the weightings of the Part scores so that each part is worth an equal number of points toward the Total. Table I presents the results of a re-analysis of the data on just such a basis (see Appendix). For convenience of comparison the correlation data from the 1971 paper is reproduced as Table II (see Appendix). Table II was actually based on 102 subjects, rather than 100, as was incorrectly reported in the earlier paper. Two errors in the data deck discovered in the re-analysis and corrected in Table I are *not* corrected for Table II. It is reproduced exactly as it was originally presented in the 1971 paper.

It is noteworthy that the re-analysis (see Table I) shows a .94 correlation between the adjusted Dictation score and adjusted Total, while the correlation between Composition and Total is reduced from .88 (Table II) to .85 (Table I). Corrections of the two errors detected in the data cards account for the slight discrepancies in intercorrelations between the Parts in Tables I and II.

The data indicate that the Dictation by itself could validly be substituted for the Total (where the Total is computed by adding the equally weighted scores on Vocabulary, Grammar, Composition, Phonology, and Dictation).

Table III (see Appendix) presents correlations with the Total scores, eliminating self-correlations of Parts in a step-wise fashion. In other words, each Part is correlated with the Total computed by the sum of scores on the remaining Parts. For example, Dictation is correlated with the sum of Vocabulary, Grammar, Composition, and Phonology. Here again we see clearly the superior performance of Dictation as a measure of the composite of skills being tested.

Together with the earlier research of Valette (1964, 1967), the follow-up research of Johansson (1974), and Oller (1972a, 1972b, 1972c), the foregoing constitutes a clear refutation of the claims by language testing experts that dictation is not a good language test (cf. Harris 1969; Lado 1961; Somaratne 1957; Anderson 1953 as cited in the 1971 paper but *not* in the references to this paper).

Moreover, the high correlations achieved repeatedly between dictation and other integrative tests such as the cloze procedure (see Oller 1972b, 1972c) support a psycholinguistic basis contrary to much recent theorizing (see *TOEFL: Interpretive Manual,* 1970) for interpreting intercorrelations of tests of language proficiency. When intercorrelations between diverse tests are near or above the .90 level, a psycholinguistic model leads us to infer high test validity for both tests. In a cloze test, for example, material is presented visually, whereas in dictation, it is presented auditorily. When such vastly different tests consistently intercorrelate at the .85 level or better (cf. Oller 1972c, and references), we may reasonably conclude that they are tapping an underlying *competence.* Since we can assume on the grounds of independent psycholinguistic research that such an underlying competence exists, we may without danger of circular reasoning argue that the two tests cross-validate each other. Obviously this will lead us to expect high intercorrelations between *valid* language tests of all sorts. Low intercorrelations must be interpreted as indicating low test validity, i.e. that one of the tests being correlated does *not* tap underlying linguistic competence or that it does so to an insufficient extent.

III. HOW DOES DICTATION MEASURE LANGUAGE COMPETENCE?

The complexity of taking dictation is greater than might have been suspected before the advent of "constructivist" models of speech perception and information processing (Neisser 1967; Chomsky and Halle 1968; Cooper 1972; Stevens and House 1972; Liberman et al 1967). The claims underlying these psycholinguistic models is that comprehension of speech, like other perceptual activities, requires active analysis-by-synthesis. "All of these models for perception ... have in common a listener who actively participates in producing speech as well as in listening to it in order that he may compare ... [his synthesis] with the incoming [sequence]. It may be that the comparators are the functional component of central interest. ..."[3] We suggest that the comparator is no more nor less than a *grammar of expectancy.* It seems that the perceiver formulates expectancies (or hypotheses) concerning the sound stream based on his internalized grammar of the language.[4] We refer to this process in the title of the paper where we suggest that dictation is a device which measures the efficiency of *grammar-based expectancies.*

Neisser (1967) posits a two stage model of cognitive processing of speech input and other sorts of cognitive information as well. In the case of speech perception, the listener first formulates a kind of *synthesis* that is "fast, crude, wholistic, and parallel"; the second stage of perception is a "deliberate, attentive, detailed, and sequential" *analysis*. We may apply this model to the writing of a dictation, providing that we remember there must be a rapid-fire alternation between *synthetic* and *analytic* processes. We may assume that a non-native speaker forms a "fast, crude . . ." notion of what is being talked about (i.e. meaning) and then analyzes in a "deliberate, attentive . . . sequential" fashion in order to write down the segmented and classified sequences that he has heard. As Chomsky and Halle (1968) suggest in another context, "the hypothesis [or "synthesis based on grammar generated expectancies," in our terms] will then be accepted if it is not too radically at variance with the acoustic material."[5] Of course, if the student's (or listener's) grammar of expectancy is incomplete, the kinds of hypotheses that he will accept will deviate substantially from the actual sequences of elements in the dictation. When students convert a phrase like "scientists from many nations" into "scientist's imaginations" and "scientist's examinations," an active analysis-by-synthesis is clearly apparent. On a dictation given at UCLA not long ago, one student converted an entire paragraph on "brain cells" into a fairly readable and phonetically similar paragraph on "brand sales." It would be absurd to suggest that the process of analysis-by-synthesis is only taking place when students make errors. It is the process underlying their listening behavior in general and is only more obvious in creative errors.

Since dictation activates the learner's internalized *grammar of expectancy*, which we assume is the central component of his language competence, it is not surprising that a dictation test yields substantial information concerning his overall proficiency in the language—indeed, more information than some other tests that have been blessed with greater approval by the "experts" (see discussion in the 1971 paper). As a testing device it "yields useful information on errors at all levels" (Angelis 1974) and meets rigorous standards of validity (Johansson 1974). It seems likely to be a useful instrument for testing short-term instructional goals as well as integrated language achievement over the long-term. There are many experimental and practical uses which remain to be explored.

NOTES

1. The paper referred to actually appeared first in *UCLA TESL Workpapers* 4 (1970), 37-41. It was published subsequently in *English Language Teaching* 25:3 (June 1971), 254-9, and in a revised and expanded form in H. B. Allen and R. N. Campbell, eds.,

Teaching English as a Second Language: A Book of Readings, New York, McGraw Hill, 1972, pp. 346-54.

2. On the other hand, Breitenstein's remarks also indicate two serious misunderstandings. The first concerns the use of dictation as a test. Breitenstein suggests, "let us not forget that in our mother tongue we can fill in gaps in what we hear up to ten times better than in the case of a foreign language we have not yet mastered" (p. 203). Ignoring the trivial matter of Breitenstein's arithmetic and its questionable empirical basis, his observation does *not* point up a disadvantage of dictation as a testing device—rather a *crucial* advantage. It is largely the disparity between our ability to "fill in gaps in our mother tongue" and in a "foreign language" that a dictation test serves to reveal.

   The second misunderstanding in Breitenstein's letter concerns student errors. He says, "the mistakes are there, but are they due to the 'dictator,' the acoustics of the room, the hearing of the candidate, or his knowledge?" (p. 203). Admittedly, bad room acoustics or weak hearing may result in errors unique to a particular student, but difficulties generated by the person giving the dictation will show up in the performance of many if not all of the examinees and, contrary to what Breitenstein implies, it *is* possible to identify such errors. Moreover, the purpose of the particular dictation Breitenstein was discussing was to measure the listening comprehension of college-level, non-native speakers of English under simulated classroom listening conditions. To attempt perfect control of acoustic conditions and hearing acuity would not be realistic. An important aspect of the ability to understand spoken English is being able to do it under the constraints and difficulties afforded by a normal classroom situation.

3. Cooper 1972, p. 42.

4. Throughout this paper we assume a pragmatic definition of *grammar* as discussed by Oller (1970, 1973a), Oller and Richards (1973). The main distinction between this sort of definition of *grammar* and the early Chomskyan paradigm is our claim that one must include *semantic* and *pragmatic* facts in the *grammar*. Also see Oller (1973b). Later Chomskyan theory has begun to take steps to correct the earlier inadequacy (Chomsky 1972).

5. As cited by Cooper 1972, p. 41.

REFERENCES

Allen, H. B. and R. R. Campbell, eds. (1972). *Teaching English as a Second Language: A Book of Readings*. New York: McGraw Hill.

Angelis, P. (1974). "Listening Comprehension and Error Analysis." In G. Nickel, ed., *AILA Proceedings, Copenhagen 1972, Volume 1: Applied Contrastive Linguistics*. Heidelberg: Julius Groos Verlag. 1-11.

Breitenstein, P. H. (1972). "Reader's Letters." *English Language Teaching* 26:2, 202-3.

Chomsky, N. (1972). *Language and Mind*. 2nd ed. New York: Harcourt, Brace, Jovanovich.

——— and M. Halle (1968). *Sound Patterns of English*. New York: Harper and Row.

Cooper, F. (1972). "How is Language Conveyed by Speech." In Kavanagh and Mattingly, eds., 25-46.

Johansson, S. (1974). "Controlled Distortion as a Language Testing Tool." In J. Qvistgaard, H. Schwarz and H. Spang-Hanssen, eds., *AILA Proceedings, Copenhagen 1972, Volume III: Applied Linguistics, Problems and Solutions*. Heidelberg: Julius Groos Verlag. 397-411.

Kavanagh, J. F. and I. G. Mattingly, eds. (1972). *Language by Ear and by Eye: The Relationships Between Speech and Reading*. Cambridge, Mass.: M.I.T. Press.

Liberman, A. M., F. S. Cooper, D. P. Shankweiler and M. Studdert-Kennedy (1967). "The Perception of the Speech Code." *Psychological Review* 74, 431-61.

Makkai, A., V. B. Makkai and L. Heilman, eds. (1973). *Linguistics at the Crossroads: Proceedings of the 11th International Congress of Linguists, Bologna, Italy.* The Hague: Mouton.

Neisser, U. (1967). *Cognitive Psychology.* New York: Appleton-Century-Crofts.

Oller, J. W., Jr. (1970). "Transformational Theory and Pragmatics." *Modern Language Journal,* 54:7, 504-7.

______ (1971). "Dictation as a Device for Testing Foreign Language Proficiency." *English Language Teaching* 25:3, 254-9.

______ (1972a). "Assessing Competence in ESL: Reading." Paper presented at the Annual Convention of Teachers of English to Speakers of Other Languages, Washington, D.C. Published in *TESOL Quarterly* 6:4, 313-24.

______ (1972b). "Dictation as a Test of ESL Proficiency." In Allen and Campbell, eds., 346-54.

______ (1972c). "Scoring Methods and Difficulty Levels for Cloze Tests of Proficiency in English as a Second Language." *Modern Language Journal* 56:3, 151-8.

______ (1973a). "On the Relation Between Syntax, Semantics, and Pragmatics." In Makkai, Makkai, and Heilman, eds.

______ (1973b). "Pragmatics and Language Testing." Paper presented at the First Joint Meeting of AILA/TESOL, San Juan, Puerto Rico. Revised and expanded version in Spolsky (1973).

______ and J. C. Richards, eds. (1973). *Focus on the Learner: Pragmatic Perspectives for the Language Teacher.* Rowley, Mass.: Newbury House.

Rand, E. J. (1972). "Integrative and Discrete Point Tests at UCLA." *UCLA TESL Workpapers* (June), 67-78.

Spolsky, B., ed. *Current Trends in Language Testing.* Forthcoming.

Stevens, K. N. and A. S. House (1972). "Speech Perception." In Wathen-Dunn, ed., *Models for the Perception of Speech and Visual Form.* Cambridge, Mass.: M.I.T. Press.

Valette, R. M. (1964). "The Use of the Dictée in the French Language Classroom." *Modern Language Journal* 48:7, 431-4.

______ (1967). *Modern Language Testing: A Handbook.* New York: Harcourt, Brace, and World.

APPENDIX

Table I

Re-evaluation of Intercorrelations Between Part Scores and Total Score on the UCLA ESLPE 1 with Adjusted (Equal) Weightings of Part Scores (n=102)

	Vocabulary (25 pts)	Grammar (25 pts)	Composition (25 pts)	Phonology (25 pts)	Dictation (25 pts)
Total (125 pts)	.79	.76	.85	.69	.94
Vocabulary		.57	.52	.42	.72
Grammar			.50	.50	.65
Composition				.50	.72
Phonology					.57

Table II

Original Intercorrelations Between Part Scores and Total Score on UCLA ESLPE 1 from Oller (1971) – Weightings Indicated (n = 102)

	Vocabulary (20 pts)	Grammar (25 pts)	Composition (25 pts)	Phonology (15 pts)	Dictation (15 pts)
Total (100 pts)	.77	.78	.88	.69	.86
Vocabulary		.58	.51	.45	.67
Grammar			.55	.50	.64
Composition				.53	.69
Phonology					.57

Table III

Intercorrelations of Part Scores and Total on UCLA ESLPE 1: *With Self-correlations Removed and with Equal Weightings of Part Scores (n = 102)*

	1 Vocabulary (25 pts)	2 Grammar (25 pts)	3 Composition (25 pts)	4 Phonology (25 pts)	5 Dictation (25 pts)
Total I (2 + 3 + 4 + 5=100 pts)	.69				
Total II (1 + 3 + 4 + 5=100 pts)		.69			
Total III (1 + 2 +' 4 + 5=100 pts)			.72		
Total IV (1 + 2 + 3 + 5=100 pts)				.59	
Total V (1 + 2 + 3 + 4=100 pts)					.85

DISCUSSION

Davies: May I make two points? The first relates to the last point that John Oller made about high and low correlations. It seems to me that the classical view of this would be that in a test battery you are looking for low correlations between tests or subtests, but high correlations between each subtest and some kind of criterion. Clearly, if as he suggests two tests are correlating highly with one another, this would mean that they would both be valid in terms of the criterion, assuming that you have a criterion. It would also mean presumably that you would only need to use one of them. Now the other point, this business of the grammar of expectancy. I find John Oller's comments very persuasive. Clearly, what we have is a test that is spreading people very widely. He didn't tell us what the standard deviation was, but I would suspect that it would be quite high, and it is essentially for this reason, I think, that he's getting the high correlations with the other tests when he groups them together. The dictation test is providing a rank order, which is what one demands from a test, and it is spreading people out. Now, this is a persuasive argument in favor of a test. Of course it isn't the ultimate one, because the ultimate one is whether the test is valid. However, he provides

think we can approximate that. Of course, as I said, even the interviews have never been validated against a real criterion. With the paper and pencil and tape recorded tests, the Defense Language Proficiency Tests, we can reliably rank them, put them in a T-scale. Since we have no way of getting access to the criterion population to get a metric from which to make a criterion-related validation of the DLPT, we are unable to say that a particular score on the DLPT represents level 2 or level 3. So we provide the information we can to the user for his purposes in deciding where to send Sergeant Jones and where to send Sergeant Smith.

Clark: The reason that I asked that question is that the achievement versus proficiency testing nomenclature might be a red herring in the sense that you really don't care whether it's an achievement test in terms of content and syllabus or a proficiency test in a sense of being able to do something for real-life purposes, because in either event, regardless of the name of the test, the ultimate validation would be against some as yet unavailable criterion.

Cartier: That would be true except for a complication that I only mentioned very briefly in the paper, and that is that the DLI courses are not the sole source of military linguists—by linguist in the military we mean a man who speaks a foreign language. They come from other sources too. A man grew up in a family where his mother spoke Serbo-Croatian, so he learned Serbo-Croatian. When he comes into the Army he claims to be highly proficient in Serbo-Croatian. We need to have some way of the finding out whether, in fact, that's true. So we have to use some kind of test to do that. Obviously the Air Force or the Army would like to have the statement we make about that man be comparable to the statement we make about the graduate.

Clark: So it would be a proficiency test for the people coming in from the outside with background knowledge, and an achievement test for those people who went through the course.

Cartier: In effect it would be, and this is a point discussed at some length in the paper. The validity of this point is one of the things that frankly we were hoping to get some ideas from you people about.

Wilds: I'm wondering if you're going to be able to extricate yourself from S and R ratings. I'm not clear if people want to know what those ratings are for your graduates, how you are going to supply them, or if you're not going to supply them, how you're going to talk people out of wanting them.

Cartier: As I said in the paper, these matters are under consideration by Headquarters DLI at the present time. I think it's premature for me to say what that decision would eventually be. We would like to be able to satisfy everybody, and maybe we'll figure out some kind of system for doing that.

Spolsky: I'd like to come back to the problem of relating the tests so closely to the syllabus. Once you're successful, you'll never be able to arrive at any satisfactory judgment of how to change either. Having a test that is independent of the syllabus will give you a chance of complaining that the test is not doing well for your students, and therefore you worry about the test; or that the syllabus is not doing well for your students, and then you'll worry about the syllabus. In other words, as soon as the two of them are based on exactly the same analysis, unless you've discovered the magic principle underlying the structure of language and how to teach it, then this kind of decision is likely to block you from getting anywhere. I think that one of the things suggested earlier was the possibility of using a test based on a syllabus, but based on someone else's syllabus, or a test based on an earlier syllabus, or a test based on a new syllabus you're thinking of having. But as soon as the test and the syllabus are based on exactly the same analysis, the best you can expect is that your students will do better on the test than students who come in from anywhere else. I think this sort of practical question, the effect on the possibility of future development of locking the two things together, is one that would worry me very much. That is why I would argue very much for a proficiency test which itself is based on some different kind of analysis. The advantage of taking an integrative approach is that it is not based specifically on any kind of analysis, and therefore remains fairly independent.

Cartier: We're concerned about this too. We very seriously considered the possibility of going to other syllabuses. The difficulty there is that I think we have the only 24-week Haitian Creole course in the world, for example. There are FSI courses for many of the languages that we teach, but the question comes up as to whether the FSI course is a rational sample for military people. An additional rationalization for the procedure that we're suggesting is that the course that we teach at DLI is more or less targeted in on the language problems of military personnel. The test is then more valid for making the personnel selections than the language sample in Serbo-Croatian that a man got because he learned from his mother or someplace else. So I think I can rationalize that if indeed our course represents the language problems of the military man more than other ways of learning the language do, then this procedure is not all that bad.

Spolsky: The more sure you are of the validity of your course analysis, the more willing you should be for your students to take tests that are unrelated to it.

Cartier: There is no disagreement at all that we would like to have a general proficiency test for use in the Defense Language program. We want to initiate research toward the criterion, and hopefully do some more research into the content domain itself.

Spolsky: But let's say you make your test and it works. You have a really good test of the present form of your syllabus, and it tests beautifully how well your students do with the material. Let's say suddenly you realize that you would like to change the syllabus. How will you justify the fact that the new syllabus produces more. You have a new test and all your students will continue to do better on this test.

Cartier: The reason for changing the syllabus would be perhaps that it's been five years since you've put it together, and a lot of the terminology has become obsolete. Another reason for changing the course might be that the Air Force wants us to place a little more emphasis on one particular language skill than we've been doing in the past, and a little less on another. Another reason you might change the course is that you find an improved methodology. If you changed the content of the syllabus, it would be for some logical reason, and that logical reason would be just as applicable to the testing program as it is to the course design. Therefore, the new test that you would have to write to represent the content of the new course would also be a valid test even for the outsider who claimed to have learned his language elsewhere, because you have changed that for operational reasons, the same reasons you change the course for.

Spolsky: And you'll be able to continue to guarantee success because you'll set the test that fits exactly what you're aiming at, and you'll prove that you get it better than anyone else.

Cartier: I certainly hope so.

Oller: I think that maybe we could suggest another kind of validity here. I don't know what one might call it, perhaps false validity. If your course is really not teaching the language, but is teaching certain things on your course syllabus, and if the test validity is related to how well the test measures what's in the syllabus, then the test could be a valid test in terms of what's in the syllabus, and still not be a measure of language proficiency. That's exactly what happens in the discrete point philosophy of testing, when you get learner grammars distorted to the point that second language learners score higher on certain items on a test than native speakers do. You train them in a way that is not really within the normal limits of the grammar of the language, but you train them in a way that has to do with how you've defined your syllabus in terms of some discrete point teaching philosophy. Then you test them on the basis of a discrete point testing philosophy, and you discover that they score even higher in some cases than native speakers do. That would be a case, I think, of false validity. Why do you have to distinguish between achievement tests and proficiency tests? People have said, if you give a proficiency test or an achievement test that's really a proficiency test, then people start teaching to the test, and with a discrete point test that can be disasterous. In the case of integrative tests it doesn't seem to be a particular problem. That is, it's very hard to improve scores on an integrative test unless you teach the language. So it seems to me that we might do well to at least challenge in our thinking the dichotomy, the dualism, between achievement and proficiency testing, and to think about the possibility that proficiency tests might be used as sort of course exit examinations, and might be used as a basis for motivating what happens in the course.

Davies: It seems to me that if one argues that a diagnostic test is a kind of non-achievement test, then in a way all achievement tests are essentially diagnostic. What one really wants to know is what people are not doing. If one is going to do anything about it, this is really what the feedback is supposed to be for. That being so, it seems to me that the value of a proficiency test in the kind of setup we heard about from Dr. Cartier is that it could be a means of validating one's syllabus. This seems to me to be particularly the value of having a test alongside the syllabus that one is using at the moment. Otherwise the syllabus is there because one thinks it ought to be there. And as we all know as language teachers, we often wonder really whether this is the right way to do things. The value of having a proficiency test alongside it is that it's one means of finding out.

Cartier: The only thing I could say to that is the same answer I gave to Bernie Spolsky, and that is, we would dearly love to have what we've been pretending to have, and that is a proficiency test validated against an external criterion, or validated in some legitimate fashion. We don't have one at the moment. The practical problem is simply that at the present time I have no access to the criterion population. And so I am proposing something that will keep us going in some kind of legitimate fashion until we can get some of the research done into content and criteria and come up with a proficiency test that we can stand behind.

Clark: You say that there are certain pragmatic and practical needs that you have to face and resolve, and I'm very sympathetic with that. I would suggest, and I think this might satisfy some of Bernard's criticisms or observations, that one of the main concerns is that the same people who are doing the course are also doing the tests. I should think that you could identify people who are familiar with the military situation, but who are not directly associated with DLI, especially not with the teaching part of it, to just take a thorough look at the test and say in their opinion if the language is the kind that the operational program requires. I think that might be of some practical help in the validation process.

Cartier: Indeed it would. We are beginning to use what we call TLA's, or technical language advisors. These are military people who have learned the language, and have gone out and used it for a number of years. They're not native speakers, but at least they know the work context. We're getting advice from these people regularly.

Petersen: We've had different linguists produce supposedly parallel proficiency tests. We administer them to the same population, and very often we find out that they don't correlate highly. I think that this is one of the problems with a definition of proficiency. It seems to depend on a particular item writer or test constructor as to what it means.

Two Tests of Speeded Reading[1]

Alan Davies

In this paper I place question marks against two current topics in the language testing literature, those of communicative competence and criterion-referenced tests. What I have to say may be construed as a criticism of "integrative" or "global" tests. It is not intended to be so. The two tests I describe in this paper *are* integrative or global and while I do, in passing, query their value, I conclude by suggesting that global tests which do not pretend to be anything else can be a proper part of a proficiency battery, and that, indeed, they may serve as a means of resolving the dilemma of choice that seems to be at issue, that of *either* norm-referenced *or* criterion-referenced, *either* content *or* predictive validity.

It is never difficult to relate developments in one branch of language study and teaching to those in another. A recent development in linguistics has been the rejection of formalism, of formal models. Grammar has moved into semantics so that the boundary, always faint, now seems non-existent. At the same time there has been a great increase in interest in all areas of macrolinguistics (Lyons 1968) and particularly since the slowing down of the 1960s' thrust in psycholinguistics (Bruner 1974) and in sociolinguistics. Hence the attempts not only by sociolinguists and ethnomethodologists but by microlinguists to look at discourse, i.e. to accept that the sentence is not the absolute upper limit of analysis.

In language teaching there has been a similar move into non-discrete and often mixed areas. Of course, *which* areas are now a matter of dispute and uncertainty. Again there has been what is regarded as a failure of formalism, the failure of the New Key and the general structural approach and the seeming inability of applied linguists to formulate how to handle the implications of generative grammars. Parallel to the interest in discourse I have mentioned has been the growing feeling that language teaching lacks situation, and here I do not mean the simple deictic language teaching situation through realia or pictures used in beginners' courses. Nor do I mean the normal—and useful—provision in courses such as English for special purposes of help with text cohesion and the various intersentential devices. Instead I think here of the need of advanced learners for an introduction to the rules of discourse, i.e. some help with the ways in which discourse can use variation as a process and fashion within-text meanings for its tokens (Widdowson 1974). Of all recent developments in language teaching this link-up with discourse analysis seems to me the most promising. It is the most concrete attempt to formalize communicative competence for language teaching purposes. However, it has serious difficulties, namely, that all attempts so far to describe discourse start from a national framework and end up in uncertainty. Speech acts and speech functions are of interest as ideas to teachers and learners, but they remain undescribed. And what is not described cannot properly be tested.

In language testing the same move and the same rejection can be observed. Already in the 1960s discrete point testing was being queried (Davies 1968). Global and integrative tests have become more attractive and are being justified under the aegis of communicative competence. It is, of course, one thing to borrow some other discipline's theory if it contains a usable formalism (e.g. psycholinguistics borrowing from T.G.), but quite another to borrow some other discipline's notions and then use them as notions once removed. Language tests cannot both test the communicative competence hypothesis and at the same time justify themselves by a theory of communicative competence.

In all these developments a two-fold argument is implicit: note that sometimes one part is made, sometimes the other, rarely both:

(1) *any* analysis is false to the truth of the language, especially any formal analysis, because it cannot get everything in, or because, simply, formal analysis is wrong.

(2) this particular analysis is false because it ignores the necessary data that has been idealised away; therefore it ignores not just what is peripheral but what is central to meaning and to language, e.g. context, variation. Typically, the grammar, the structural and transformational drill, the discrete point test item have accepted the need for idealisation, i.e. they have been selected as exemplifying features of *linguistic* competence. The existence of a gap between them and the behaviour they are intended to represent has always been admitted, even indeed Lyons' (1972) discussion of idealisation accepts the existence of and argues the need for such a gap in linguistics.

The move away referred to above is not just the consequence of fashion, nor does it reflect a distaste for formal analysis. It is rather a consequence of the failure, real or not, of these models, namely the linguistic one does not satisfy the canons of scientific respectability; the teaching one does not succeed, students and teachers get bored and learning stops; the testing one is abandoned because of knock-on effects from both the others and because it claims to have (and indeed may have) more concern about its validity than either of the others.

Formal models may have been abandoned, where they have been, for the right reasons; but it is difficult to see, if we now concentrate on the testing field, what is to take their place. Presumably communicative competence: the difficulty here is how to work idealisation in reverse, i.e. to hold constant for the linguistic parameter, just as the linguist holds constant (by standardisation, by decontextualisation) for the sociolinguistic parameters. Or is it to be the global test? It is surely significant that along with the development I have indicated has gone an awakened interest in cloze procedure and the dictation technique, both global in their approach.

I want now to turn away from movements and look at some examples of tests. About 10 years ago I constructed an English Proficiency Test Battery (EPTB, Davies 1967) on behalf of the British Council who have since that time made use of the Battery in a number of countries as a means of assessing the English proficiency of students applying to the Council for scholarships, etc. in order to study in the United Kingdom. Most of the students tested were until fairly recently postgraduates, but latterly the test has also been used to select people applying for technical assistance awards, many of whom will be attached for their training to institutions and organisations other than universities. For a considerable period the Battery existed in only two versions (A and B), but last year Alan Moller, a Council officer, and I worked together to produce a C version. The reworking and rewriting led me to consider afresh the structure of the Battery and recall the original design.

The rationale I adopted in 1964 was twofold: the Battery should have a linguistic base and a work sample base. This led eventually, after elimination of subtests, to a four-part Battery: (1) Phonemic Discrimination; (2) Stress and Intonation; (3) Reading Comprehension; (4) Grammar. Numbers 1 and 2 were on tape; 3 and 4 were written. There was also a fifth test—(5) Reading Speed—which has been used as an optional extra. It is of Tests 3 & 5 that I want to speak: these two represent what remained of my work sample selection. Tests 1, 2 and 4 represented the linguistic sampling and were, I suppose, discrete point tests, inasmuch as it seemed clear what was being tested in each item, a phoneme contrast in 1 or a modal contrast in 4. It was, admittedly, less clear in Test 2; and I sometimes wondered if Stress & Intonation did not belong more properly to the work sample selection. Stress and Intonation are notoriously difficult to pin down as discrete markers of contrast. But at the time it did not seem to matter too much which side of the fence Test 2 belonged on since it seemed happily settled on top of the fence. What did matter was that Stress and Intonation were part of the language, areas of linguistic investigation, and they appeared to pose problems to advanced learners of English. So the work sample tests proper remained: Test 3, Reading Comprehension, and Test 5, the optional test of Reading Speed.

Sampling of the language is, of course, the chief burden placed on the proficiency tester; it becomes also his main strategy since it determines, other things being equal, what he tests. If it is a problem for discrete point tests (where to some extent the sheer accumulation of items lessens the weight of decision on the tester), how much more so for the work sample test where practicalities such as time make accumulation of items impossible and the tester's decision final. Now it so happens that in any test very few texts can be employed as exemplars of critical work samples. Of course, as we all know, there are ways around this dilemma. The first is through "ideal type" selection, a kind of content validity, in which the tester recognises a particular text as being exactly what he wants, representative of all possible texts for his population. Such an approach is, of course, guesswork, but not uncommon. The other way out, usually employed in addition to the first, is through correlation, either of the concurrent or of the predictive kind. Here the tester discovers that his text sampling does predict after all, a fortunate outcome and one he is glad to accept since he is usually not also an experimenter who would be seeking texts with better and better predictions. Work sampling, then, in the choice of texts is a form of guesswork. The guesswork may be confounded by yet more guesswork in the method employed to assess comprehension of the text, whether it be written or spoken.

At this point illustrations of Tests 3 and 5 would be in order:

TEST 3

This is a Test of your understanding of written English. Here are 2 passages taken from fairly recent books. In each passage a number of the words are shown only by their initial letter and a dash. Complete these words to show that you understand these passages.

Here is a short example:

T............ i............ a test o............ reading comprehension

If you read the whole sentence you will see that it makes some sort of sense but that three of the words are incomplete. Try to complete them. Have you succeeded? They are: *This*, *is* and *of*. Thus the complete sentence reads: This is a test of reading comprehension.

Now go on to the two questions below. Work quickly.

Question 1

But........... changes i............ t............ home are less revolutionary, a............ easier t............ assimilate, t............ changes i............ industry. Technical progress h............ removed only part o............ education f............ t............ home; long after either she o............ her husband has ceased t............ be one f............ their son, t............ mother is f............ her daughter a teacher w............ accustoms her t............ a particular way o............ doing things i............ t............ home, a .... t............

daughter, s............ her ways are also her mother's, is likely t............ feel t............ she can trust t............ good sense o............ her helper.

Question 2

I............ is f............ t............ reason t............ India became t............ first area t............ encounter t............ problem o............ using English a............ t............ commercial, educational a............ scientific medium i............ w............ are now called 'under-developed' countries: a problem w............ became acute b............ t............ middle o............ t............ twentieth century i............ many parts o............ t............ world.

TEST 5

Our British policy for *speak* higher education is tenable only *girl* on certain assumptions. The first did assumption is that the numbers yes of young people selected each year shouldn't for the nation's needs weather. The third assumption our is that we offer acceptable opportunities whiten for part-time further education to grudge those who are not selected. None of these assumptions the is justified. Our eighth methods of selection assume that our who intellectual resources are limited old by genetic factors, and that when snake we select candidates to monumental go to grammar imagine schools or to universities we are drawing from the population reclining those with the innate ability to thighs profit from these privileged for kinds of education. Of course, the I intellectual resources sketch-book in a population are ultimately limited by its fifty genetic make-up. But we have if abundant evidence that it is not ten genetics, but inequalities in previously our society and inadequacies in our educational than system, which at present limit as our investment in man; and didn't this is true driftwood even in the most affluent nations. Mental there is now convincing evidence that idea thousands of has children fall out of our handle educational system each year prefer not owing to lack hard of ability but owing to ag lack of motive, and incentive, and pelvis opportunity.

*The text of Tests reproduced here contains about 1/5 of the total test.

Test 3, as you can see, is a variety of cloze test, but it differs from classical cloze in three ways: first, it is speeded, i.e. testees are given 5 minutes to complete closure of the 49 items; second, the initial letter of each item is given (and only original, writer's words accepted); third, the items do not represent every nth word but a random selection of function or grammatical words.

If, as I have suggested, prediction is to be the touchstone for a global test, then indeed Test 3 predicts, with considerable variability in the size of correlation. However, satisfactory figures ranging from .4 to .7 have been achieved for different populations, using either end-of-course results or tutors' assessments of English as the criterion. Again, it has satisfactory internal statistics, reliability (various) ranging from .8 to .95, a mean of 27, and an s.d. of 13 (A version). Its correlation with Test 5 for a variety of populations is always between .5 and .7. It is a practical test which is grasped easily by the testees and is very quick to administer.

What, however, is it testing? It is labelled Reading Comprehension, but then any test that is not a spoken one is likely to be a reading test of some kind. Test 3's r of .5, .6, .7 with Test 5 has been quoted. What does Test 5 measure? As you can see, the technique here (after the practice lead in with the non-English words) is to interpose English distractors randomly in a running text. Testees are asked to mark (circle) these distractors while "reading" the text as fast as they can. They are stopped at the end of 10 minutes, and the number of distractors located is their raw score. There is a deduction for each non-distractor marked (but not more than 4 deductions in any one line of the original text). Again, the validity figures against the same criteria have the same range (.4-.7) as Test 3. Its range of rs with Test 3 has already been quoted. Its reliability has always been above .9. Its mean is 70, and its s.d. is 33 (A version).

Does Test 5 test reading speed? There are two other pieces of evidence—one old, one new. The old one refers to the relation of both Tests 3 and 5 to Test 4—my discrete point grammar test. This test has 47 items, is of the multiple-choice variety (3 choices), and is traditional in format. Its validity rs have again a similar range—.4-.8—with the same criteria as Tests 3 and 5. Its range of rs with Tests 3 and 5 is .5-.7. We can say, therefore, that the mean r between Tests 3-4, 4-5, and 3-5 is .6. Test 4's reliability is between .8-.9 (A version), its mean is 33 and its s.d. is 8 (A version). The first bit of evidence I mentioned is that, in the original Factor Analysis Tests, 3, 4 and 5 all loaded on the 3rd Factor, which was labelled Reading Comprehension. But I do not wish to press this point, since they also loaded on the 1st Factor, along with other tests, and because one of the tests of listening comprehension also loaded with them on the 3rd Factor (though, as usual, it was possible to wriggle out of this embarrassment by pointing to the literary nature of that particular listening text and to the amount of reading comprehension involved in answering the multiple-choice questions).

The second piece of evidence is recent. The new interest in cloze procedure has not passed us by in Edinburgh, and this has led one of our postgraduate students who is interested in the place of literacy among secondary school students in Botswana to construct two cloze tests, one in English and one in Setswana. It has also led us to ask ourselves what a cloze test tests. Further, it led me to speculate as to why I had bent the cloze technique, and I found I could not remember, except that it seemed (and still does seem) practical. But in an attempt to gain some impression of the effect of speeding on my Test 3, I recently carried out a small experiment using both the A and C versions of Test 3 in a crossover design. I gave the speeded version first to a group of mainly African student teachers (N 21). The result was, along with a massive gain in mean score (well over one s.d.), an r of just under .6. This is not surprising since it has been estimated elsewhere (see Cronbach 1964) that nearly 40 percent of the variance in a speeded reading test may be accounted for by speed alone. In my case it could well be more. This is not surprising, but it is curious, since I now have the paradoxical situation in which Test 3 (speeded but labelled Reading Comprehension) correlates .6 with Test 5 (Reading Speed), but Test 3 (speeded and now labelled Reading Speed) correlates .6 with itself (unspeeded and now labelled Reading Comprehension).[2] It would seem, therefore, that we have not only different kinds of reading comprehension but different kinds of reading speed, too. Cronbach (1964) offers some comfort here: "Reading development includes both speed of reading and comprehension, and a useful test must consider both these elements. Most testers have tried to measure the two aspects of performance independently, but they have been largely unsuccessful." So Test 3 could be regarded as a perfectly proper global test containing reading speed and reading comprehension.

But if there is some doubt as to the influence of the speed factor in Test 3, what of the comprehension? Opinions differ on cloze procedure. Both Weaver and Kingston (1963) and Rankin (1957) have raised experimental doubts, while Schlesinger (1968) has raised the more theoretical question as to whether cloze can be more than a means of assessing awareness of intersentential relations. Bormuth (1969), Oller and Conrad (1971), and Oller (1972a) have reported results to the contrary, with Bormuth showing very high (.95) correlation with multiple-choice tests. Satisfactory results have also been reported for L2 learners (see Bowen 1969; Oller 1972a and b). It seems that while cloze tests do test something related to language, i.e. some aspect of reading, it seems equally clear that we do not know what they test. As Carroll (1972) and Schlesinger (1968) ask, the latter directly, it's time in reading research to measure not just "how much" has been understood but also "how much of what."

Eventually we always come to the question of what tests are for. The purpose of a test, as opposed to, say, an exercise, is to provide a rank order. Hence, as I see it, the need for criterion-referenced tests to be at bottom, for some populations, norm-referenced. The dispute between norm- and criterion-referencing seems to me to be about samples and populations rather than about content and criteria. (Of course, it is both, but for any given test, criterion-referenced for one sample, there is always a population available on whom the test could be norm-referenced.)

But there is no need to force so severe a division. Since the assumption with an ability is that it is known differentially, this presumably means that learners know different bits. The chief way, then, of determining what should be included in a test is content sampling, i.e. by content validity. And this seems to me exactly what criterion-referencing is on about. What is more, it seems to me exactly what discrete point testing was on about, too, since the assumption was that the language was describable into those units and those bits. It is, of course, true that the proficiency tester makes up his syllabus as he goes along so that, although there is no known syllabus for him to sample as content, he does have his parallel, assumed syllabus. Global tests, integrative tests, cloze, dictation, reading speed, and the like work essentially on predictive validity. But predictive validity (or concurrent validity since they are essentially the same) is a poor substitute for content validity, since it puts all the onus of decision on the criterion, and it is well known how unreliable (and often invalid) they are. And, of course, grades for foreign students often sink to an r of .2 with an English language predictor; tutors' assessments are of more value, but an r of even .6 (which is by no means unsatisfactory) is really very small when you remember how much of the variance, all of which in this case is language, is unexplained.

This is not an attack on figures. Rather it says we must work to get meaningful ones. Discrete point tests *are* useful in proficiency batteries, since they give a point of reference and enable us to make use of content validity. Global tests (i.e. cloze) *are* useful in proficiency tests, since they can be validated by means of predictive validity. Furthermore, for a given sample of testees it might be possible to make use of content validity in selecting a series of texts for global testing. Here we see the possible marriage in global tests of criterion-referenced and norm-referenced testing. (Admittedly, if the sample is "given" and homogeneous, we might be more honest to describe this as an achievement test). Finally, I should like to see work develop quickly in two areas. First, instruments (i.e. rating forms) should be constructed for valid criteria; this would meet my point of getting hold of meaningful figures. Second, in the area of validity I have not mentioned the most powerful of all validities, construct validity—most powerful because it derives from theory. Here is exactly where communicative competence experimentation needs to be done.

Communicative competence is the primary ability to be tested. We should regard it as similar in development to language aptitude, and thus, when we come to construct tests of communicative competence, we use construct validity to justify our items. This means that we have to be clever, cleverer than in writing cloze items. But it also means that we do not perhaps need to wait, as I suggested earlier, on description before trying out our first experiments as long as we maintain the proper difference between the purpose of a test and the purpose of an experiment.

NOTES

1. I am grateful to Alan Moller and Dan Douglas who have helped me with some of the ideas presented in this paper. Responsibility for the paper, however, is entirely mine.
2. "Speeded reading" is a not entirely satisfactory cover term for both Tests 3 and 5. Test 3 is a speeded test of reading. Test 5 is a test of speed reading. Hence the title which attempts to bring both tests under one label.

REFERENCES

Bormuth, J. R. 1969. "Factor Validity of Cloze Tests as Measures of Reading Comprehension Ability." *Reading Research Quarterly* 4:3, 358-365.

Bowen, J. D. 1969. "A Tentative Measure of the Relative Control of English and Amharic by Eleventh-Grade Ethiopian Students. *UCLA Workpapers in TESL* 2, 69-89.

Bruner, J. 1974. "Language as an Instrument of Thought." In A. Davies, ed., *Problems in Language and Learning.* London: Heinemann.

Carroll, J. R. 1972. "Defining Comprehension: Some Speculations." In J. B. Carroll and R. O. Freedle, eds., *Language Comprehension and the Acquisition of Knowledge.* New York: Halsted Press.

Cronbach, L. J. 1964. *Essentials of Psychological Testing.* New York: Harper and Row.

Davies, A. 1967. "The English Proficiency of Overseas Students." *British Journal of Educational Psychology* 37:2, 165-74.

———. 1968. "Introduction." In A. Davies, ed., *Language Testing Symposium: A Psycholinguistic Approach.* London: Oxford University Press. 1-18.

Lyons, J. 1968. *Introduction to Theoretical Linguistics.* London: Cambridge University Press.

———. 1972. "Human Language." In R. A. Hinde, ed., *Non-Verbal Communication.* London: Cambridge University Press, 49-85.

Oller, J. W., Jr. 1972a. "Scoring Methods and Difficulty Levels for Cloze Tests of Proficiency in English as a Second Language." *Modern Language Journal* 56:3, 151-8.

———. 1972b. "Controversies in Linguistics and Language Teaching." *UCLA Workpapers in TESL* 5, 39-50.

——— and C. A. Conrad. 1971. "The Cloze Technique and ESL Proficiency." *Language Learning* 21:2, 183-95.

Rankin, E. F. 1957. "An Evaluation of Cloze Procedure as a Technique for Measuring Reading Comprehension." Unpublished Ph.D. dissertation. Ann Arbor: University of Michigan.

Schlesinger, I. M. 1968. *Sentence Structure and the Reading Process.* The Hague: Mouton.

Weaver, W. W. and A. J. Kingston. 1963. "A Factor Analysis of the Cloze Procedure and Other Measures of Reading and Language Ability." *Journal of Communication* 13:4, 252-61.

Widdowson, H. 1974. "Stylistics." In S. P. Corder and J. P. B. Allen, eds., *Edinburgh Course in Applied Linguistics, Volume 3: Techniques in Applied Linguistics.* London: Oxford University Press.

DISCUSSION:

Oller: John Clark said yesterday in regard to cloze tests and related tasks that this behavior would rarely be called for in normal language situations. I think that's true only in the case of the kind of cloze tests that Dr. Davies used and the kind described in the Bondaruk paper. The problem there is that the blanks are spaced too close, and it becomes, I think, more of a puzzle solving task. It gets progressively farther and farther away from the sort of thing that people normally do in conversational use of language. You do, of course, occasionally supply words when you're listening, and the same kinds of things happen in reading when you run across an unfamiliar word, for example. Research with native speakers has shown that spaces closer than every fifth word generate a lot of items that even native speakers cannot answer. So that one would expect it to change the properties of the task fairly substantially with non-native speakers as well. And for that reason the .4 to .7 correlations that Dr. Davies has observed are not particularly surprising to me, and in fact I wouldn't expect you to be able to get much better than, say, a .7 correlation with that type of test unless it has some characteristics that would controvert research that's been done with native speakers. I also have a second comment concerning sampling techniques. It seems to me that the idea that you can adequately sample language in the traditional sense of the term, or the notion of sampling in statistics, is really inappropriate. I think, rather, that what we ought to be doing is trying to challenge or test the efficiency of some internalized grammar. There's an infinite number of possible English sentences, and any test is an insignificant sampling of them.

Davies: In answer to the first comment, I never claimed that my type of cloze test is intended to be a direct test of behavior in the sense that this is what people actually have to do. But as I tried to argue this morning, I don't think this is what most tests do in fact. There always has been a gap between what is presented and what is expected, what it is meant to represent in some way. The fact that I present items that may occasionally come more than 5 spaces apart is, I think, unimportant, since the initial letter is given, which makes a very remarkable difference, obviously cutting down chance by a considerable amount. Also, I have quite carefully determined that native speakers in fact score at least 95 percent correct on this test. I don't mean approximations, but original words. I don't think that I would accept your criticism at this point on those grounds as being a very strong one. As far as the correlation is concerned, again .4 to .7 is, remember, a correlation of each of these tests with some kind of predicted criteria which sometimes came at the end of a whole year of study. So that's a long time to be predicting anything. My point of quoting the range of correlations is to indicate that sometimes they were better, sometimes they were worse. There were worse ones than those also, but they were always insignificant. It is, after all, a battery of tests. If one of my tests had been predicting at the level of .85, I would have abandoned the other tests in the battery. But since it is a battery, the multiple correlation that they adapt to does sometimes reach about .8. As to the other question about sampling, I take your point about the infinity of possible sentences in English. However, this does not prevent either linguists or teachers from assuming that they are talking about the language in some way. If they appreciated the vastness of infinity, then it seems to me they would both give up because they would feel that they would never get anywhere. But people don't do that. They assume that they are getting somewhere and that what they're about is meaningful in terms of the language. What they're doing is sampling, and the success of what they're doing is determined by the appropriateness of the sample they take.

Oller: It seems to me that the basis for the kind of cloze test that you've done, Dr. Davies, is kind of discrete point philosophy related to the notion of sampling techniques. I think that's your basic argument against the integrative or overall global proficiency type of test. But there is a fundamental problem with the sampling theory that assumes that even though a task is horrendous and very long, that one should go ahead and tackle it anyway with relatively primitive tools. That is, if there is an infinite number of twenty-word sentences in English, then to tackle that task by any kind of procedure that assumes listing and sampling of items from a list is not only a primitive method, but one that is essentially unworkable, I think. The alternative afforded by integrative testing, or by what Spolsky speaks of as global proficiency testing, is to assume that the learner is internalizing a grammar that itself possesses properties which enable it to cope with an infinitude of sentences. Somebody suggested this morning that people have competencies that involve samples of language. I think that's really not true for native speakers, who are capable of understanding just about any sort of English whether they've ever heard it before or not. We don't really go about memorizing samples. These two philosophies of testing, and of what language proficiency consists of, are different in a very fundamental and deep sort of way. I think that it's important to make that distinction.

Davies: It seems to me that your philosophy is that of a direct test. What you really want is to get hold of some behavior that somehow is in direct equivalence to what the learner is, as you put it, internalizing. It seems to me that this is not necessary, though, as I pointed out at the end of my paper, it can be of use. I don't think, however, one should assume that this is the only way in which one can test.

Cartier: When you're faced, as I am, with the necessity of deciding whether Sergeant Jones or Lieutenant Smith has some degree of skill in Russian or Persian or whatever it may be, you have to figure out some system by which you can report to the Air Force or to the Army something about that. In order to do that, I have to make something that will be called a test. And regardless of what I do, it's necessarily going to be a sample of his linguistic behavior. Also, John Oller pointed out that native speakers have something more than a sample of the language. If you've ever talked to a lawyer about a court decision or a contract or something, you know for a fact that his sample of English differs from yours. This is also true for pilots and for cab drivers. I happen to believe that is a part of the English language, but it is a special sample that that person has, and I suggest that each of us has, along with his own idiolect, his own special sample of the language at large.

Spolsky: It seems to me that we're using the term sample in two senses and for two different purposes. One, we're using it in the general sense, that is, a sample is something selected out of something and obviously any test has to be a selection out of the total universe. Second, we're using the term sample as it's defined and used within certain kinds of statistics to justify the fact that a sample represents the whole.

Oller: I think that one way of describing this other kind of sampling is that you have to ask people to do something with language which gives you some information about what kinds of language situations they are capable of responding in. Instead of thinking about taking a bunch of items out of a potential universe of items, you think in terms of the underlying grammar that is appropriate to the situations that you're trying to put the learner into in order to find out how well he handles the language of those situations. In other words, how efficient is his grammar rather than how representative is your sample of some list. We ought to be sampling or testing or measuring or challenging the efficiency of the internalized grammar. If we start thinking in those terms, we formulate, I think, a substantially different set of questions than we do if we think in terms of trying to find a representative sample out of a list or universe of discrete items of some sort.

Davies: Yes, but the trouble with your argument, as I found it not only in regard to my paper but in previous discussion also, is that you seem to be wanting to use your test not merely as a means of testing this internalized grammar, but of finding out what it is. It seems to me, therefore, that you're trying to do two jobs with the same thing, and I don't think that's satisfactory.

Oller: Suppose you do find out some fundamental things about the nature of the grammar. I would say more power to you if you can. And if at the same time you also do a better job of finding out what level of proficiency the student is at, again, more power to you.

Davies: It seems to me that you're justifying, as I understand it, the selection of a text for cloze procedure on the basis that any text is as good as any other. It seems to me that, if pushed, you would not in fact agree that that is the case, and that you would have to admit that you sample in some way. And then I would ask you on what basis you sampled.

Oller: If we're talking about testing for instructional purposes, and most of us are interested in it from that point of view as well as from the other research angles, I think we can assume that the classroom teacher has a minimal amount of intelligence about what level of language is appropriate to that class of students. The person who is admitting foreign students at the university level has a pretty good understanding of the kinds of language skills that would be appropriate to those foreign students. One would construct a listening comprehension test that was appropriate to the sorts of things that would happen in university courses.

Problems of Syllabus, Curriculum and Testing in Connection with Modern Language Programmes for Adults in Europe

Gerhard Nickel

This paper reports mainly on work and research undertaken by the Council of Europe in Strasbourg with a view to developing a unit/credit system for modern language learning by adults. This system, of course, urgently requires a set of tests, large in number, adapted to the different aims and objectives of the learners.

Beside the so-called objective tests, some of the classical tests like composition and translation are likely to be retained within this system. Among other topics, therefore, I shall briefly discuss the possible role of translation within the system. Finally, I should like to touch on urgent problems connected with language testing which should be tackled prior to devising tests, including the evaluation and grading of errors made by learners of foreign languages. There appears to be more interest in this problem in Europe than in other parts of the world. As I stated in my paper at the 24th Annual Georgetown Round Table, "The future of Europe requires the imperfect polyglot rather than the perfectionist. . . ." (Nickel 1973b:183)

Integration and mobility of population within Europe must be promoted through increased foreign langauge learning, particularly among adults, since schools have, on the whole, already intensified efforts to teach foreign languages. Intensifying language teaching is closely linked with the strengthening of motivations. Motivation again depends heavily upon breaking down a global concept of language teaching into units and sub-units, combined with the close description of language needs in Europe. These needs must form the basis for devising courses, tests and examinations. Thus, a multi-dimensional classification of learners' needs should provide a framework for the content, type and standard of tests and examinations, already existing tests as well as new ones. In order to establish potential equivalences within Europe and between Europe and other continents, the tests and examinations should be monitored and constantly evaluated.

Before devising these teaching and testing units, one must undertake a classification of situations in which the languages are to be used by the learners. This classification may utilize different parameters. A number of classifications have been set up in the United States by different agencies, the most commonly known being the U.S. Civil Service Definitions for Language Proficiency. Without attempting to hierarchize the system of parameters, I think the following are worth mentioning: situation, number, role, time, place (including "macro-place," e.g. countries). A further attempt to describe learners' needs in the light of situations in which the foreign languages will be used has been based on socio-professional data. The latter very often combine with socio-cultural data. Thus, for instance, a scientist will certainly be expected to know enough scientific items in the target language (TL) to be able to understand, speak, read and perhaps even write in his special field. Sometimes, however, he will only need a passive knowledge of the language. On the other hand, his socio-cultural ambition may motivate him to acquire a larger or smaller part of the general vocabulary of the TL so that he will be able to discuss a variety of subjects outside his field.

An example of language achievements which can be aimed at within a specific vocational framework, that of a qualified business secretary, has been presented by Trim (1973:27). His list is an open-ended one which will certainly vary from firm to firm and from country to country, and it may be affected by other factors. It shows clearly how many situational and linguistic tasks a secretary is confronted with.

If we consider the many kinds of situations in which languages may be used and the various kinds of socio-professional and socio-cultural motivations which may be operative, it becomes quite obvious that different linguistic levels exist and that the finding of a so-called "threshold level" will be quite a difficult matter (van Ek 1973:95).

During the past few years the German Confederation of Adult Education Colleges *(Volkshochschulverband)* has developed basic programmes in several langauges with minimal vocabularies for English, French, German, Russian and Spanish ranging from about 2000 to 2500 items each, with the aim of establishing minimal language programmes for these languages. It has since become obvious, however, that programmes containing fewer items and even simpler structures should also be made available for certain learners (tourists, migrant workers who have just entered the country, etc.).

What is becoming increasingly frequent in Europe, particularly at European committee meetings, is the use of two or even more languages in discussions. Speakers use their mother tongues or other languages which they assume their hearers will be able to understand, and are prepared to be addressed in a different language by other speakers using their mother tongues or idioms with which they are familiar. This, of course, creates a new situation, which may well have to be taken into account one day in devising language programmes including language tests of different bilingual types.

Where language tests are concerned, two general courses are open to us: tests can be devised for given language courses or language material or courses can be designed for given tests. The former approach is the more popular one in Europe at present. The latter is not infrequently used by some governmental agencies in the U.S. This means that a considerable number of tests of different types will have to be designed which take into account all the various parameters mentioned above. There is little doubt that in addition to short time-saving tests of the so-called objective type (I prefer the term "tests with reduced subjectivity") such as those of the multiple-choice kind, the old classical type of tests involving composition and translation will be retained in spite of all the criticism in the past.

It is very interesting to look at the history of the role of translations in language teaching and testing. While translations originally formed part of the so-called "translation method" (whatever that meant), their pedagogical value outside the field of translation was sometimes questioned on the grounds that translating is a "highly complex skill [requiring] special talent and special training" (Lado 1967:261; Valette 1967:162). Translating is undoubtedly an art, but so is writing essays and compositions. The choice of simple and more "concrete" texts can reduce the expertise required and therefore simplify the procedure. Just because translating is such a complex activity which encompasses several skills, it has, I think, greater value from a diagostic point of view than some other tests. All the so-called four skills are complex. Therefore, I am sure that future test systems in Europe will also include passages of translation. Swedish universities, for instance, which have abolished translations in their state final examinations have now discovered that a very important parameter for testing higher skills has been thrown overboard both to the regret of teachers and many students. Translations may, therefore, be reintroduced into the Swedish university system.

Supervision-investigations into the achievements of German students at universities where I have taught have indicated that on the whole there was a closer correlation between the marks given for written translations and oral performance in the TL than generally has been assumed. As we all know, we have not yet investigated fully enough the connections that may exist between passive and active skills and particularly between non-speaking skills and the skill of expressing one's self orally. Additionally we do not know enough yet about the correlations between the different skills, and we have certainly been overrating the disparate nature of the different skills. It also became clear to me that translating constitutes a clearer distinguishing parameter among higher marks than do other tests.

There are many ways of defending and justifying a given type of test if the text is simple enough and does not make sufficiently high demands on the testees' non-linguistic skills. One should, where possible, make use of realistic, down-to-earth texts such as those in middle-class journals and newspapers.

Another argument in favour of translations is that they often have to be made in a given cultural context, at least where the European cultural context is concerned. As examples one could start with the wording on road signs, public warnings and the like, and move on to the situation where short passages from newspaper articles, advertisements and other brief items have to be translated for acquaintances, friends, tourists, etc. Here translations correspond to real-life situations. This criterion, of course, does not offer anything new and considers the value of translations within their own scope. Reliability, validity and objectivity of these translation tests are necessarily increased if the text is relatively simple. Needless to say, there is an increasing demand for good translators and interpreters in Europe, but the specialized techniques they have to learn are taught at special schools.

Other factors have contributed to the rise in popularity of translation texts in the recent past. A consequence of foreign-language instruction, geared to individual needs, of contrastive linguistics, and of modern learning psychology, with its growing emphasis on the cognitive aspects of learning, is that applied linguists no longer insist on a monolingual approach to foreign language learning, and the limited direct confrontation with mother tongue elements is no longer considered harmful (Butzkamm 1973; Altmann 1972; Levin 1973; Politzer 1968; Beck 1974). The use of mother tongue elements, which includes the presentation of TL rules, does not seem to interfere with the acquisition of the TL. Thus, a very important argument against using the mother tongue as a metalanguage in FL teaching seems to me to have lost some of its weight. This certainly does not mean that intensive use of the mother tongue within FL teaching is to be advocated.

What is more, from a contrastive point of view a confrontation with the mother tongue may reinforce one's knowledge of rules of the TL. One of the tasks of language testing is certainly to test the amount of interference taking place between the mother tongue and the TL. Not all types of learners will make more interference mistakes when translating than when writing an essay or a composition, but undoubtedly some groups of learners will. However, there is a correlation between the number of interference mistakes and the kind of test depending upon the type of learner (Nickel 1971:225). Multiple-choice tests, for instance, seem to elicit fewer interference mistakes than tests assessing the active use of language. Psycholinguistic aspects like stress, nervousness and depression and sociolinguistic features like inhibition, which very often shows itself also in the use of the mother tongue (lack of motivation, etc.), are some of the factors distinguishing individual forms of behaviour, as is shown in the amount and type of interference between the mother tongue and the TL. If one of the tasks of the test is to measure interference, then translation should not be dismissed from the group of tests as a whole.

As has been pointed out by other scholars, the translation of mother tongue sentences into the TL has as a testing technique certain advantages over purely TL tests involving completion and transformation of utterances. Thus, an example like *my/pyjama/be/red* [may] tempt some pupil to make errors that could scarcely be made elsewhere: **My pyjama is being red*, **My pyjama are being red*, **My pyjamas are being red /! /* are in my experience all possible answers to this kind of test, yet I doubt if any of them would occur if the printed word *be* had not occurred in the formulation of the test. In addition, it may be said that the formulation of a TL question usually involves highly unnatural and often semantically strained language" (Mathews-Breský 1972:59).

Here we encounter a clear methodological disadvantage of monolingual tests. It is also apparent that certain tests produce and elicit certain kinds of errors, and we must make sure whether a particular kind of error is due to a particular kind of test or whether it is really an "all-round" error on the competence level.

Thus, I have tried to show in this paper that there are several reasons to support translation as one type of test. These reasons, by implication, range from the psychological via realistic (translation for its own sake) to the contrastive and even to the sociological type.

One problem that in my view has not received sufficient attention anywhere in the world, and which certainly will have to be looked into closely in connection with the previously mentioned European scheme, is the question of error evaluation and error grading. It is undoubtedly in this area that more objectifying is called for. On the whole I think we have been talking more about tests than about the grading of errors. I believe, however, that a discussion of how to grade errors should precede the devising of tests or at least be carried on parallel to test designing. Error grading on its part will be closely linked up with learners' objectives, needs and motivations, to name only some factors involved. This problem certainly cannot be solved by linguists alone, since errors also have pedagogical implications. We should endeavour, however, to set up a hierarchy of the factors relevant to this issue. The following four parameters have been suggested among others: (1) degree of acceptability; (2) degree to which the communication act is distorted by the error; (3) significance in the process of teaching and learning; (4) degree of difficulty encountered by learners. It has also been suggested that acceptability should be given priority over the factor of communication distortion (Legenhausen 1974).

In the light of what I said previously, this kind of hierarchization cannot be considered an absolute one. Undoubtedly, with lower "thresholds" communicability should be given priority over acceptability. Native speakers all over Europe will have to accustom themselves to applying less rigorous standards of linguistic correctness when confronted with various kinds of non-acceptable but clearly decodable statements (Nickel 1972). The hierarchization I have just mentioned may, of course, be used at a college or university level, where higher degrees of proficiency are called for. It should by now be clear that a very important point in connection with language testing will be the problem of setting up norms and standards of correctness. This is a very significant point which is integral in establishing the degree of validity of tests. Even ungrammatical and unidiomatic forms may be deemed correct at certain testing levels and completely incorrect at other levels. This is particularly true with low threshold levels in connection with basic communication at a very simple level.

It is also quite clear that error marking should never be done by non-native speakers working by themselves but only in cooperation with native speakers, since there are enormous divergences between native speakers' and non-native speakers' judgments concerning errors. Naturally there are divergences also among native speakers and among non-native speakers due to attitudes towards language uses and language norms acquired in connection with their mother tongue learning. Native speakers, for instance, who have stayed away from their home-countries for a long period have very often antiquated views on present-day usage. These views, by the way, are also often reflected in teaching materials produced by them. If all these factors are overlooked, tests of all types, and not only translation tests, become quite unreliable and of little value.

The fact that a given error may be due to interference between target languages or between one TL and the mother tongue should not cause us to draw the false conclusion that this is necessarily a serious error. Other factors have to be taken into consideration, too. Thus, error evaluation and grading is of great importance for the assessment of tests (Nickel 1973:9).

I am convinced that the highly complex certification system for language teaching, particularly where learners are adults, will involve an equally complex set of tests incorporating different views on error evaluation. In spite of the complexity of the nature of errors, where linguistic, sociological, communicative, pedagogical and other aspects are involved, one should attempt to increase the objectivity of language testing by trying to describe errors and their significance in an objective manner at different stages of learning with various types of tests and in communication situations.

In connection with this certification system, all kinds of tests will have to be considered. Some of the classical and less objective types like translation will have to be re-considered from the point of view of psychology, contrastive linguistics, real-life situations, sociolinguistics and other factors. Looking at the matter from the point of view of psychology, I am convinced that quite a few speakers of foreign languages formulate their TL utterances via silent translations, though perhaps they do this subconsciously. This may also be true with other tests like cloze testing, where some learners may also use silent translations for help.

REFERENCES

Butzkamm, W. 1973. *Aufgeklärte Einsprachigkeit.* Heidelberg: Quelle and Meyer.

Lado, R. 1967. *Language Testing.* Reprint. London: Longman's.

Legenhausen, L. 1974. *Fehleranalyse und Fehlerbewertung.* Unpublished Ph.D. dissertation.

Levin, L. 1973. "Comparative Studies in Foreign-Language Teaching." *The GUME-Project.* Stockholm: Almquist and Wiksell.

Mathews-Breský, R. J. H. 1972. "Translation as a Testing Device." *English Language Teaching* 27:1, 59-65.

Nickel, G. 1971. "Problems of Learners' Difficulties in Foreign Language Acquisition." *International Review of Applied Linguistics* 9:3, 219-228.

______. 1972. *Fehlerkunde: Beiträge zur Fehleranalyse, Fehlerbewertung und Fehlertherapie.* Berlin: Cornelsen-Velhagen und Klasing.

______. 1973a. *Testen: Probleme der objektiven Leistungsmessung im fremdsprachlichen Unterricht.* Berlin: Cornelsen-Velhagen und Klasing.

______. 1973b. "Needs and objectives of Foreign Language Teaching in Europe." In Kurt R. Jankowsky, ed., *Georgetown University Round Table on Languages and Linguistics 1974.* Washington, D.C.: Georgetown University Press. 179-186.

Sepp, B. 1974. *Die Rolle der Ubersetzung in Fremdsprachenunterricht.* Unpublished M.A. thesis.

Svartvik, J., ed. 1973. *Errata: Paper in Error Analysis.* Lund: CWK Gleerup.

Trim, J. L. M. 1973. "Draft Outline of a European Unit/Credit System for Modern Language Learning by Adults." In *Systems Development in Adult Language Learning: A European unit/credit system for modern language learning by adults.* Strasbourg: Council of Europe. 15-28.

Valette, R. M. 1967. *Modern Language Testing.* New York: Harcourt, Brace and World.

van Ek, I. A. 1973. "The 'Threshold Level' in a Unit/Credit System." In *System Development in Adult Language Learning: A European unit/credit system for modern language learning by adults.* 91-128.

DISCUSSION

Lado: I think translation as a test of translation has a certain amount of face validity. It's the business you're engaged in. Therefore, when you use translation to test translation, the validity questions are: is it a good sample of translation, is it an appropriate sample, and so on. However, when you use translation as a test of speaking, then you have a problem of face validity because translation is different from speaking. Therefore, the burden of validation is to find out whether this test of translation correlates highly with a valid test of speaking. If it does, then you can use it. If it doesn't, then you can't. I would like also to contribute some of my research in a series of experiments on language and thought. In one of the experiments I had subjects do immediate translation, and an equivalent group of subjects did, if you want to call it, delayed translation. They took some time in between. The number of errors of various types of those who did immediate translation was 3 to 1 higher than those who were asked to retranslate with a time delay between the two. And this was in both directions, going from L1 to L2 or going from L2 to L1. When you're forced to do immediate translation, your immediate memory is in full operation because you can retain a phrase in immediate memory and you tend to go from surface structure in L1 to surface structure in L2 or vice versa. This increases the complication.

Nickel: I don't think we disagree basically. First of all, I've also noted the difference between immediate and delayed translation. Secondly, in the terms of the validity we have the same problem in connection with any other kind of testing, and I wonder whether the correlation between multiple-choice tests and other tests is much higher than between these tests and translations. If my assumption is correct, more speaking is done via some kind of subconscious underlying and silent translation, and translation is underlying lots of testing performance. I'm really pretty well convinced that we have been underrating the amount of translation that is being done in practice. This is, of course, an assumption that we have to prove, and I don't want to give you the impression that I'm in favor of a mass translation test, but rather a battery of tests with one of the exams a translation. I'm also in favor of some kind of guided translation, where certain rules and hints are given.

Oller: I agree with the idea about translation, and just wanted to call attention again to important research which showed that the kinds of errors people make in translating from the native language into the TL are precisely analogous to the kinds of errors they make in spontaneous speech in the language, and also in imitating fairly long sequences of information in the TL.

Rashbaum: I'd like to ask Dr. Nickel what specific criteria were used in that translation test, and what were the weights attached to them, ranging from grammar, lexicon, and the fluency of the style of translation?

Nickel: We have not yet set up concrete tests which have official acknowledgement. We envision tests where lexis will be given priority over grammar, for instance for migrant workers staying only a short time in European countries. At higher levels we will give acceptability priority over communicability, but there will be other groups of learners where we will have priority of communicability, including a certain weighting on vocabulary.

Concluding Statement

Bernard Spolsky

One of the best ways to try to sum up this Symposium is to consider the four questions that Randall Jones set for us at the start of the Symposium and examine how well we have answered them.

The first question that he suggested we consider was the state of the art of language testing in the United States Government. He made it clear how difficult it would be to make any changes, but urged us to propose any improvements that we considered worthwhile. I think we touched on some important aspects of this question. First, there was our intensive discussion of the Foreign Service Institute's oral interview. Most language testers have a deep respect for this test but are usually frustrated by the lack of published description and discussion of it. I know of only one article dealing with it at any length, and even that is quite brief. Presumably, there is a good deal of internal documentation, and there has surely been a great deal of in-house discussion. But I know of no opportunity before this meeting for academic testers to discuss it in public with the Government testers who are working with the technique. It was very helpful, therefore, to hear Claudia Wilds' paper and to listen to the discussion that followed. The doubts raised about the validity of the scale and about the sociolinguistic limitations of the formal interview, with the consequent questioning of its predictive validity for other situations, are healthy and useful. We reached no conclusions, but the discussion that started was a fruitful one. It was particularly encouraging to find that, with all the great investment of time and effort that has gone into the oral interview, there was no suggestion that it was not still open to debate and improvement.

A similar openness was obvious in the other statements by members of the Government testing community. When the testers from the Defense Language Institute and the Department of Defense proposed new techniques or expressed concerns about validity, they did so with a degree of scholarly tentativeness that any academic researcher would be proud of. That is to say, there were no signs that Government language testers were set and smug about their existing programs or certain that any new ones they were working on would be perfect solutions to their problems. They showed both concern for what works and interest in fundamental principles. In this situation, I think we can answer Dr. Jones' question by saying that language testing in the United States Government is alive, inquisitive, and healthy.

His second question was whether there were common problems for various members of the testing profession. We did very well with problems, even if we could not agree on any solutions. Here, I think a number of useful and interesting contrasting trends became clear in the course of the meeting. There was the usual contrast between those who want to know what they are going to do tomorrow to test 3,000 employees about to be sent overseas, and those of us who ask what a language test really is. But we generally did well in balancing the theoretical and the practical. A second, more theoretical, argument ran through the meeting: the old question of discrete point versus integrative tests. With most of the big guns now on their side, the integraters have not yet squelched some discrete practitioners. A third interesting struggle was kept beneath the surface most of the time: the sometimes completing claims of psychologists and linguists, each with their own conception of what language testing should be. Of all fields in which testing is used, language testing is, I believe, the one where the subject matter specialist does best. It may have been a result of the proportion of linguists to psychologists at this meeting, but I think that it is a fair reflection of what is happening in the field. Linguists are, in fact, easily interested in such testing questions as the distinction between proficiency and achievement (related to competence and performance), the sociolinguistic questions of how a direct test differs from an indirect one, and the common problem behind all this, that of validity: how do you know what areas of linguistic or communicative competence you are measuring and which do you want to measure anyway? That is to say, our practical problems tend to be common to all language testers; our theoretical ones tend to unite language testers with linguists.

The third question that Randall Jones raised was whether there are any new ideas or techniques in testing. New is, of course, a relative term. There were a lot of things said or suggested here that might have seemed surprising twenty years ago, but few that would not have fitted into the 1967 Michigan meeting (Upshur 1968). Some of the questions raised there were discussed here: the basic question of what does it mean to know a language and the question of whether one tests for knowledge of items or rules. Another question raised at Michigan, and under-represented here because some of the scholars invited weren't able to come, was the sociolinguistic aspect of testing. What does it mean to test communicative competence? What is the influence of the testing situation itself? We didn't raise many new questions, nor did we propose new techniques. Indeed, some ideas with new names turned out to be old techniques in different contexts.

There are some new techniques we didn't hear much about, such as those involving communication tasks, but we can guess that if they had been described, they would have turned out to be something tried in British West Africa in 1897 and never before referred to in print!

The fourth question we were set was to suggest directions for future research and development. There are two kinds of research strategy that we seem to agree are most necessary. The first is to test a small group of subjects with a great variety of techniques, so that we can find some way of deciding the relationship between the variable kinds of measures that are used. The second is to try certain techniques on a great variety of subjects, so that we can consider the interaction of subject and technique, looking, for example, at the relation between the subject's learning history and the test technique.

There is another area in need of attention that I should mention here, that of terminology and definitions. The fact that most of us come from language teaching or linguistic backgrounds means that we do not have to accept standards of terms or tests such as those set up by the American Psychological Association. And as linguists, we assume that we either take part in the writing of dictionaries or that dictionary makers record our usages. But we should still be careful of the way we use words. Very often, we were talking about the same thing but using different terms, as when Clark talked of face validity and Davies of content validity, or when Oller talked of cloze tests and Bondaruk and his colleagues of contextual tests. And quite often, we were probably referring to different things when we used the same terms. The more we have meetings and discussions like this, the more chance we have to understand each other's special terminology, or to come to agree on standardization.

There are three areas in which research is clearly going to be important. The first might be labeled the psycholinguistic area, where the concern is to understand what it means to know a language. The basic question of the distinction between discrete point and integrative tests might be considered here.

The second is the psychometric and statistical. Language tests in general and global or integrative language tests in particular raise some very interesting statistical problems. Knowing a language appears to be different from knowing a lot of other things. Linguists believe this, and will keep on saying it to each other whether anybody else will listen to us or not. But if we are right, then testing knowledge of language and testing knowledge of other things should turn out to be different in crucial ways. Most of the statistical and psychometric techniques used within the various fields of testing seem to assume that you have to handle lots of discrete items and find ways of pulling them together. There are, however, good reasons to believe that, in the case of language, one is dealing with sizable or complete chunks; rather than having to pull them together, one assumes that the togetherness is there but needs to be explored. It was particularly interesting, then, to find a statistician pointing out the existence of problems like these and suggesting that new kinds of statistics will be needed to handle the special problems of language tests.

The third area requiring a great deal more research than any of us talked about is the sociolinguistic aspect. A first question here is what a direct measure really can be. The criticism of the FSI oral interview was not that it fails to measure how well people perform in a formal interview, but to what extent a formal conversational interview might predict other kinds of real language behavior. We need, therefore, the kinds of definitions that sociolinguists are giving us of various aspects of communicative competence, and we need to know how one might go about sampling from the various situations. There are already quite a number of clues to the answer to that question in work on bilingualism, where the concept of domain turns out to be a very useful construct for lumping together large areas of different situation, role, and style. It may well be that when one tests for real-life situations, Fishman's work with domains might turn out to be a way around the enormous task that Gerhard Nickel suggested when he talked of listing all the possible linguistic situations in which a person needs to perform. We will also need to face up to the problems of style and register testing that are involved.

I think these are more or less the answers we gave to the questions that Randall Jones set for us; whether or not he will be satisfied that we have answered them is another matter. As an extra question of my own, it would be reasonable to ask, "How might such research be done?" I am reminded of the distinction sometimes made between applied and basic research. It goes something like this: basic research is what you want to do; applied research is what they will give you money to do. I believe we have seen at this Symposium a display of a field in which there is a very useful connection between the practitioner who can get money to do something and the theoretician who is asking basic questions. This tie between practice and theory, whether money is involved or not, is, I believe, why linguists find language testing such an intriguing field. The theoretical questions, the basic questions that need to be solved if useful tests are to be produced, are very similar to the theoretical questions that need to be solved to understand language. That is to say, developing a good measure of language competence is very close to understanding what language is, or, put another way, the problems of language testing turn out to be very serious challenges to our understanding of what language is. There is, therefore, an extremely useful relationship set up at a meeting like this between those of us from universities who tend to worry about basic issues and those in the practical world who need to produce workable tests. It is very useful for the two groups to come together, to notice common problems, and to notice that ultimately the solution to the practical and the theoretical problems will come at the same time, whenever that may be. There is not the very strong division between theory and application that we sometimes seem to feel when we first start talking to each other.

I would like to take this opportunity, then, to thank the sponsors of this Symposium, to thank the Government agencies for inviting the Commission on Language Testing to join with them in setting up this meeting, to thank Georgetown University and the Center for Applied Linguistics for their work in making the meeting possible, and to thank the audience who patiently listened to our discussions and raised new questions for us to consider.

List of Contributors

John Bondaruk is a Research Psychologist with the Department of Defense, where he is currently Chief of Personnel Research and Testing.

Francis A. Cartier is with the Office of Research and Development of the Defense Language Institute, which is responsible for development of courses and tests in the over 40 languages taught to personnel of the U.S. Armed Forces.

James R. Child is a designer of language aptitude and proficiency tests for the Department of Defense and works on a contract basis as a translator of Turkish, Hebrew and Indonesian for the World Bank.

John L.D. Clark is Senior Examiner in Foreign Languages at Educational Testing Service, Princeton, New Jersey, where his principal responsibilities include coordination of test development for the Test of English as a Foreign Language (TOEFL).

Alan Davies is on the faculty of the University of Edinburgh. His principal interest is in language testing.

Harry L. Gradman is an Assistant Professor of Education at Indiana University. He is currently on leave from Indiana and is Visiting Assistant Professor of Elementary Education and Adviser to the Program in Linguistics and Language Pedagogy at the University of New Mexico as well as Co-director of the Navajo Reading Study.

Peter J. M. Groot is presently at the Instituut voor Toegepaste Taalkunde, Riiksuniversiteit te Utrecht, The Netherlands and is Cochairman of the AILA Commission on Language Tests and Testing.

Randall L. Jones is Assistant Professor of Linguistics and German at Cornell University, Ithaca, New York. His main interests are in language testing and the teaching of reading in a second language.

Gerhard Nickel is Director of the Institut für Linguistik: Anglistik, Universität Stuttgart and serves as an advisor to the Council of Europe and UNESCO and as Secretary General of the Association Internationale de Linguistique Appliquée (AILA).

John W. Oller, Jr. is the Chairman of the Department of Linguistics at the University of New Mexico. He is particularly interested in the integrative and pragmatic procedures of language testing and in the area of psycholinguistics in general.

Calvin R. Petersen is with the Office of Research and Development of the Defense Language Institute. He is a specialist in the fields of clinical and research psychology.

Bernard Spolsky is Professor of Linguistics, Elementary Education and Anthropology at the University of New Mexico as well as Co-chairman of the AILA Commission on Language Tests and Testing.

Virginia Streiff is currently a Ph.D. candidate at Ohio State University. Her major interest is in the general area of educational linguistics.

Emery W. Tetrault is a Language Researcher for the Department of Defense. He is an applied linguist whose main interest is in foreign language testing.

Claudia P. Wilds was formerly Associate Director of the Psycholinguistics Program at the Center for Applied Linguistics. She has long had contacts with the Foreign Service Institute (FSI) and currently works at intervals on projects at FSI which are related to language proficiency.